WITHDRAWN

POLITICS
THE
CONSTITUTION
AND THE
SUPREME
COURT

An Introduction to the Study of
Constitutional Law

Loren P. Beth
University of Massachusetts

HARPER & ROW, PUBLISHERS
New York, Evanston, and London

POLITICS, THE CONSTITUTION, AND THE SUPREME COURT:
An Introduction to the Study of Constitutional Law. Copyright © 1962 by
Harper & Row, Publishers, Incorporated. Printed in the United States of
America. All rights reserved. No part of this book may be used or reproduced
in any manner whatsoever without written permission except in the case of
brief quotations embodied in critical articles and reviews. For information
address Harper & Row, Publishers, Incorporated, 49 East 33rd Street, New
York 16, N.Y.

[Quotation on page 24 by permission of The Harvard Law Review Association,
Copyright 1952.]

LIBRARY OF CONGRESS CATALOG CARD NUMBER: 62-4791

Preface

The purpose of this book is quite specific. It is the result of thirteen years of teaching constitutional law in the political science curriculum of American universities. These courses as generally taught have two primary characteristics: they use (in one degree or another) the case study method, patterned after the law schools; and the students ordinarily have little or no background in American law or the American court system. Whether the case study method is really appropriate to the study of a political science course is a matter of opinion, and perhaps in any case its effectiveness depends on the skill of the teacher. But the case method used on students without the proper background is likely to produce students who know cases but not principles, who can cite facts but cannot state the reasons for them, who know what the courts do but not how or why they do it. In short, the system produces all the effects one expects of emphasis on results to the exclusion of knowledge of theory or of the ways in which the results are achieved.

This little book is the product of years of experiment in trying to orient students to the subject of constitutional law. The author ordinarily uses at least five weeks of a one-semester course covering the materials included herein. It is to be hoped that the time needed will be shorter as a result of this book's availability. The rest of the course uses the ordinary case approach, seasoned by a judicious selection of readings. The book is, therefore, useful primarily as a supplement to the usual case or text materials used for the constitutional law course. It may also be useful as supplementary reading in other courses, such as American government or the law school course in constitutional law.

v

The approach of the book is frankly nonlegal. It emphasizes the things that the political science student should know about our judiciary: the role it plays in our political system, the reasons why it has been given such a role, and how it performs. Law students would not be harmed by exposure to this approach, even though some of their professors may view it with distrust.

An author always hopes that his work is distinctive enough to achieve some general circulation beyond its use as text material, but most of us must reconcile ourselves to the essentially esoteric nature of our work. In this case, there is no comparable work on the market, so laymen interested in our judicial system may profit from its use. It is deliberately written in nontechnical language and should be easily understood by any intelligent reader.

While I have attempted to present fairly subjects that are often extremely controversial, I have not tried to conceal my own opinions where I have them. I believe this is more honest than a pretended objectivity, and more fair to the reader. I hope that I have succeeded in making statements of opinion clearly identifiable as such, both so that the reader will not accept as definitive statements that are far from certain, and so that he may have the high privilege of arguing with me rather than nodding sleepily over a soporifically balanced presentation of both sides.

I have absorbed ideas from many people in the course of this writing, and it is almost impossible to give their original sponsors credit, since these ideas have become part of my intellectual stock-in-trade. I would nevertheless like to thank two people who have played particularly large roles in one way or another. Chief of these has been Professor William C. Havard, now of Louisiana State University, who has not only made many suggestions in the course of the work, but who has served as a brother-confessor and a sounding board for new ideas. I have sharpened my wits in a perhaps futile effort to meet the views expressed in many writings by my friend Wallace Mendelson of the University of Texas; my intellectual debt to him is no less great because I still find myself in basic disagreement with his position. Neither these unwitting helpers, nor others unnamed, bear any responsibility for the result.

Loren P. Beth

Amherst, Massachusetts
March, 1962

Table of Contents

Table of Cases

CHAPTER I

Constitutionalism
and the
American Constitution

Have you a precedent of this commission?
I believe, not any.
We must not rend our subjects from our laws,
And stick them in our will.

—SHAKESPEARE, *Henry VIII*

Man since the ancient Greeks has pondered the problem of how to reconcile the need for order and authority in society with the desire for individual liberty. In the eighteenth century Alexander Hamilton stated the problem in his famous lines from *The Federalist*: "In framing a government which is to be administered by men over men, the greatest difficulty lies in this: you must first enable the government to control the governed; and in the next place oblige it to control itself." In all societies governmental power is necessary: it serves the triple functions of maintaining domestic order, protecting against external threat, and organizing affairs and advancing the social welfare. These are all ends which most of us agree are desirable as well as necessary, and it has usually been concluded therefore that power to accomplish them is also desirable as well as necessary. Yet the experience of mankind has indicated that power is at least as likely to corrupt its holders as to ennoble them. The ideal ruler has always been he who exercises power responsibly, with the aim of achieving the ends summarized above, and with few or no personal motivations in doing so.

1

There are two reasons why we have often taken this attitude of distrust toward irresponsible power. One is obvious: that power used for personal ends is not likely to accomplish the purposes for which government is created. The other is that mankind has always had a longing to be free in addition to being well governed. It is true that this longing for freedom appears more prominently in some societies than in others—notably it has been a factor in the history of Western civilization. It is also true that there are times when other values are placed ahead of freedom. Nevertheless a constant factor in Western political thought has been the idea that a government which deprives its citizens of large amounts of individual liberty is not a good government.

Consequently a great deal of thought and political inventiveness has gone into the attempt to create political systems that will allow governments to exercise all the power that is necessary to achieve the collective ends of the society without at the same time destroying the liberties of individual members of that society. Attempts to institutionalize such a social condition are usually called *constitutionalism*, the concept of limited government.

Constitutionalism in the Ancient World

This idea of government, limited in its powers yet able to achieve social ends, is as old as the conscious study of politics; it goes back at least to the ancient Greeks in the period of philosophical speculation which gave the world its first great political thinkers—Socrates, Plato, and Aristotle.

Beyond doubt the Greeks had some conception of an outside standard by which the acts of government might be judged. In Plato, this was the ideal conception of nature, which man was expected to approximate; in Aristotle, it took the form of an emphasis on the validity of custom and tradition; and there was also the older popular feeling that the gods prescribed the normal modes of behavior. The Athenians even developed a species of popular review of governmental acts; any decision of the Athenian Assembly could be contested in the popular court through the use of a writ alleging (in substance) that the decision in question was contrary to the spirit of the constitution. This, however, was not judicial review: the Athenian court in reality was a sort of popular legislative chamber when it considered the validity of laws. Review was based on no express documentary provisions, nor was it limited by a case system.

The Greeks apparently developed only the first and most basic idea contained in constitutionalism: the concept of a standard by which acts of government can be judged as to their quality. They failed to take the next step of converting this idea from a mere criterion of the excellence of a government to a real test of its legitimacy. In other words, Greek constitutionalism went no further than to set up an intellectual standard; one might thus say that a particular government was a bad one, but this did not invalidate the acts of that government nor absolve the citizen from the obligation of obedience. The only recourse of citizens was actual revolution—a drastic remedy and one that was frequently used in the Greek city-states.

Roman constitutionalism took this second step of adding to a standard of judgment a standard of legitimacy. This was accomplished by making the people's will a guide to the validity of governmental acts. Roman constitutional theory made the people the source of all law, and no law in Republican Rome was presumed to be valid until it had been approved by the representatives of the people. Even in the Empire (although in actual fact the will of the Emperor became law) lip-service was paid to the principle. That Caesar's will did become law illustrates the fundamental defect of Roman—indeed of all—constitutionalism: the failure to develop any institution that could *enforce* the standard of validity. Most of the later history of constitutionalism is a chronicle of the attempts to find an enforcement method.

Medieval Constitutionalism

The difficulty caused by the lack of effective sanctions against government is illustrated clearly in medieval political thought. Medieval institutions were deeply constitutional, and constitutionalism was so ingrained as to be taken almost for granted. But nowhere in medieval thought was there any attempt to construct a system of sanctions (unless divine punishment be considered a sanction).

Medieval institutions were founded upon the idea that the prince was limited in his power, and that the limits were imposed by God and the ancient customs of the realm. Divine limitations arose, of course, out of the Christian faith and the idea of a universal divine law. In Christian thought, that government seemed best which most nearly governed according to the will of God. No matter how absolute the power of the ruler might be in earthly practice, it was always limited by God. This was constitutionalism in the sense that there was a standard for judging the legitimacy of governmental acts. However, not until the Reformation did there arise any general concept of what could be done *on this earth* if a ruler transgressed divine law. "Leave him to Heaven," said most medieval political theory. The effectiveness of divine sanctions imposed only after death depended on how much the ruler feared such sanctions, and how badly he wanted what he could get by transgressing. This kind of sanction (if indeed it can be called a sanction at all) could not be imposed upon the ruler from any earthly source save his own conscience, except in those instances in which the political power of the Papacy was greater than that of the ruler.

The peculiar nature of the Germanic law out of which much medieval law came was also significant. This was tribal law, handed down largely unwritten from generation to generation. The theory was that it had always existed and that it never changed. Consequently, a decree by the monarch was, theoretically if not actually, merely a statement of the law, not a creative act. "It is not for judges to judge of the law but according to the law," said Augustine; the Middle Ages applied this statement to kings. An example is provided by an edict issued by Rothar, king of the Lombards, in the seventh century. The king declared that the edict was established "by inquiring into and recalling to mind the ancient laws of our ancestors which had not been written." The inquiry was conducted not by the king alone, but with the help of "ancient men"; and it was confirmed by the assembly "according to the rule of our nation" to stand forever "for the common good of all men of our nation."

Such limitations, however, were largely theoretical; they often meant in practice little more than the king wished them to mean. There was, it is true (in Britain and France in the later Middle Ages), a twofold distinction in the types of governmental power which later became extremely important in the growth of constitutionalism in England. In essence, this distinction was an attempt to separate the legitimate powers of government from the legitimate rights of the private citizen. The oldest and most securely established of these rights, dating at least to 1215, was the right to trial by certain established procedures in criminal cases. The essential point in this distinction was that *within its proper sphere* the power of the king was conceived to be absolute; but he was legally bound not to transgress the sphere of private right. There might be *moral* limitations of the king's power in his own sphere, but the king could legally disregard them: they were self-imposed and he was a free agent—though a good king would, of course, observe them. However, in the field of private rights there were bounds to what the king could legally do; he was bound by his coronation oath to proceed by law and by no other way. The medieval distinction between autocracy and despotism consisted in this —the autocrat was a king who observed the legal limits to his power, no matter how arbitrary he might be within his own sphere; the despot was a ruler who ruled without law, simply applying his own will, even in the area of private right.

It is again true that this distinction, clear in theory as it may have been, was not effective in fact. The only actual limits to the power of the medieval monarch were his own conscience and the power that might be opposed to his by the nobles, the Church, or the people. *Magna Charta*, the first great document of English constitutionalism, was forced on the king not because he bowed to legal argumentation, but because the barons had more power than he did. The legal case may have been a good one, but it was the power that counted.

The Growth of English Constitutionalism

While the theory described above was held in England from at least the twelfth century on, it was not until the century-long struggle against Stuart absolutism in the 1600's that any effective means of checking governmental power was found. Even the means then found have proved to be only partially effective.

The struggle between parliament and the king in the seventeenth century produced the three great attempts to circumscribe governmental power. The first of these was to force the government to be responsible to the governed. At first this meant the responsibility of the king to parliament—a goal largely achieved by 1689. But parliaments might also be arbitrary and tyrannical; and so responsibility eventually was conceived to be the responsibility of the government—including parliament—to the people, through democratic representation. This, obviously, was not a real solution to the problem; for if the people ruled, they might impose what Alexis de Tocqueville, when he studied the operations of American democracy in the 1830's, called "the tyranny of the majority." The idea of self-restraint must still be relied upon, but now instead of the conscience of one man—the king—or one assembly—parliament—we must rely on the conscience of the entire citizenry. In the initial period, then, the people could force responsibility on the government, but can they, in the long run, force it on themselves? This is the unanswered question on which the future of democratic constitutionalism depends, for neither of the other solutions to the problem of sanctions can work in the absence of the exercise of responsible attitudes by citizens.

There is a second constitutional method of limiting government with which this analysis is not directly concerned, but which has been (and still is) so important in American concepts of constitutionalism that it cannot be ignored. This is the attempt to limit government by the institutional balancing of one group against another, which we know as the "separation of powers." Often referred to as the concept of "mixed government," this theory was prominently developed in the political thought of the Greeks, but even more so in the later Hellenistic period. In practice, unfortunately, the mixed state has never worked for long, because one group always gained enough power to overbalance the others. Thus the ideal does not square with the practice; Polybius' and Cicero's descriptions of Roman institutions as exemplifying mixed government were as fictitious, even when written, as Montesquieu's similar interpretation of British government centuries later. American constitution makers, however, derived their ideas from Montesquieu and Locke and other English writers of the seventeenth century, and consequently the concept of separation of powers found its way into our federal and state constitutions. It is not, all things considered, a necessary part of constitutionalism.

The third kind of attempt to enforce constitutional limitations was judicial review. While it remained for the United States to develop judicial review to the highest point, the role of courts in England provided certain important precedents. Particularly in the field of the common and criminal law, the English courts early developed a certain amount of independence from the king, and various cases can be cited to illustrate the courts applying the rules of law even against the wishes of the monarch. Perhaps the best illustration is *Cavendish's Case* (1587),[1] in which the justices of the Court of Common Pleas stood out against a direct order, several times repeated, of Queen Elizabeth, saying that it was "against the law of the land, in which case it was said, no one is bound to obey." Such judicial statements were not frequent, however, and even when made were largely ineffectual, for the judges owed their seats in court to the monarch. By the time the judges were made independent in tenure (1701), the major threat to constitutionalism was no longer the king but the parliament. Thus judicial review never became accepted in England, but the idea of its use was carried by the English to their colonial settlements in the New World, there to bear fruit.

Constitutionalism in the American Colonies

Due to the circumstances of colonial rule in the seventeenth and eighteenth centuries, such as the distance from home, the difficulty of communication, and England's inexperience with colonial government, a great deal of independence was allowed the American settlements. Colonial government was normally self-government for most internal affairs, exercised under London's authorization which was often written in the form of a *charter*. The major addition to constitutionalism during the colonial period was the growth of the use of the charter as a limitation on the powers of government. While it is true that the limitations were usually imposed by the English government in London rather than by the people themselves, colonists early became used to judging the acts of their governments (and those of the English government as well) by reference to the terms of their charters. The writing of the American Constitution in 1787 thus was merely a logical continuation of a custom already as old as the Mayflower Compact.

The political ideas used by colonists to justify the revolt against

---

[1] *Cavendish's Case*, Court of Common Pleas (1587); Anderson's Reports, I, 152, translated in James Bradley Thayer, *Cases on Constitutional Law* (Cambridge, Mass.: Charles W. Sever, 1895), I, 12–15. Also see 123 Eng. Rep. 403.

English domination included a large admixture of constitutional doctrine. A most prominent argument was that the King and Parliament had violated the constitutional rights of Englishmen, and that the violations were so serious as to call for revolution. One of the clearest statements of constitutionalism was made by that radical patriot, Samuel Adams, who maintained:

. . . That his Majesty's high court of Parliament is the supreme legislative power over the whole empire; that in all free states the constitution is fixed, and the supreme legislature derives its power and authority from the constitution, it cannot overleap the bounds of it, without destroying its own foundation; that the constitution ascertains and limits both sovereignty and allegiance.

Similar sentiments were expressed by many a budding American patriot.

As to the sanctions for constitutional principle, colonial and revolutionary thought contained all three of the sanctions we have heretofore noted. The very idea of revolution is a consequence of the concept that popular sentiment is a proper means of enforcing constitutional restrictions, and the idea of popular consent to governmental acts was thus more highly developed in revolutionary theory than ever before in human history. The second sanction—the balancing off of group against group in an attempt to prevent usurpation of power by any—was also prominent, although not so much so as it was later to become. Most of the revolutionary state governments, as a matter of fact, far from using separation of powers, came pretty close to legislative supremacy in their reaction against the colonial governors.

The third sanction, judicial review, was anticipated in the writings of many revolutionary spokesmen. James Otis was particularly prominent in this regard. "If the supreme legislature errs," he said, "it is informed by the supreme executive in the King's courts of law. . . . This is government! This is a constitution!" In addition to such statements of constitutional theory, there were various practical anticipations of judicial review, but it is sufficient here to point out that by the time the United States Constitution was written—and even more obviously by the time of *Marbury* v. *Madison* (1803)—the principle of judicial review was well known even to its opponents.

Colonial and revolutionary thought, however, is probably most important to the development of constitutionalism because of its use of the written charter as a basic law. The sanctions of constitutionalism are always difficult to use and make effective, but without a written document the difficulties are even greater.

Written Constitutions and Constitutionalism

The theory of constitutionalism does not require a written document called a constitution. As a matter of fact, the review of its history presented above indicates that there is no necessary connection at all. England, having perhaps even today the most constitutional of all the world's governments, has neither a written constitution nor judicial review. The explanation for this phenomenon seems to lie in the modern character of the British people. As Charles McIlwain remarks, the limits on arbitrary rule have existed for such a long period and have become so customary and traditional that they are observed almost as a matter of course. The doctrine of parliamentary supremacy held in England, for instance, is predicated on the tacit assumption that there are some things no Parliament would ever do. If Parliament were ever to exercise all the powers it presumably has, these powers would no doubt swiftly be taken away from it by some sort of constitutional act of the British people, or at least an attempt would be made to do so. Further, alongside the idea of the legal supremacy of Parliament has been developed the conception of the political supremacy of the electorate, a popular check which helps to preserve the constitutionalism of that country.

In America, on the other hand, government had to be set up almost overnight. It could not be built up out of the accumulation of centuries of precedent and tradition: a going society had to be governed (or, more significantly, thirteen going societies had to be brought together and governed). Considering the tradition of written charters discussed earlier, it was a logical development for Americans to perform this task of creating a government through the use of a written document setting limits to its powers. Since judicial review and thus constitutional law would probably never have developed in this country without such a written document, it is obvious that the use of a written constitution is of supreme importance to the study of constitutional law.

A written constitution is also important because of its fundamental character. In essence a constitution is an act of the people, not an act of government; in fact it *creates* a government. This creative act of the people (whether or not it literally takes place) has the result of making a constitution a fundamental document that must be observed by the government created by it, and further, of making the constitution itself unalterable by the government. It is alterable only by a special process which represents the same authority that wrote the original document—the people.

If a nation is democratic, this word "people" means all the people, whereas in a nondemocratic nation it may merely mean those people who have political rights, acting presumably for everyone. But democracy does introduce certain complications in constitutional theory, which because of their significance must be treated separately.

Constitutionalism in the American Constitution

The foregoing brief review of the history of constitutionalism in the Western world before the adoption of the American Constitution may serve as a background for some judgments as to the nature of that document, which William E. Gladstone called "the most wonderful work ever struck off at a given time by the brain and purpose of man." We have seen that constitutionalism evolved over the centuries as an idea of limited government, based on four subconcepts: a standard of moral judgment, a standard of legitimacy, a system of sanctions, and a written charter. Let us now investigate whether, and how, these subconcepts were embodied in the Constitution of the new nation in 1787.

Whatever criticisms one may practically make, the Constitution must be theoretically regarded as an act of the American people. Its framers certainly so regarded it, and the continuous acceptance of the document by most Americans ever since indicates that it has been generally so regarded. In considering the Constitution in relation to the existence of a standard of moral judgment the assumption that it embodies the consent of the people is important, for it means that the people have raised a standard representing their concept of *what government should be like*: a moral judgment about the rule of man over man. The clearest statement of this is contained in the preamble, which briefly states the aims that the American people had in mind:

> We the People of the United States, in Order to form a more perfect Union, establish Justice, insure domestic Tranquility, provide for the common defence, promote the general Welfare, and secure the Blessings of Liberty to ourselves and our Posterity, do ordain and establish this Constitution for the United States of America.

One should also keep in mind that the prevailing political theory at the time the Constitution was written included a deep belief in natural law, and that it was customary to regard the Constitution as an embodiment of the principles of that higher law which was presumed to be a standard by which human law could be judged. One might render this idea into more modern terms (since we no longer have the same overtly expressed belief in natural law) by saying that the Constitution represents the sober and considered judgment of the American people as to the political aspects of a good society. It has been our version of what is good and true in matters political. Thus it follows Aristotle's bidding that "rightly constituted laws should be the final sovereign."

But ideas of truth and justice change with changing times: if a constitution is to endure it must also change. The amending process recognizes this need for change, but it also recognizes (by making amendment difficult) that such changes should be made only when the same sober and considered judgment can be obtained which led to the adoption of the original document. Within the terms of the Constitution, as we shall see, most adaptation takes place through the expansive possibilities of general phraseology and judicial review.

The second major strand of constitutionalism is that of a standard of legitimacy. The American Constitution obviously was framed by men who were used to thinking in terms of such a standard. It is explicitly provided that only laws "made in Pursuance" of the Constitution shall stand with the Constitution itself as "the supreme Law of the Land." Consequently, all governmental acts must be judged by reference to the Constitution; and any that are not consistent with it are presumed to be illegitimate—or in the more common phrase, unconstitutional—and thus at least theoretically null and void, not morally or legally binding on the people. Just *how* such judgment of unconstitutionality is to be made in practice is not made clear in the Constitution, but that such judgment *is to be made* is exceedingly clear. In considering this question, Alexander Hamilton lucidly stated his belief in the legitimacy idea in the following words:[2]

> There is no position which depends on clearer principles, than that every act of a delegated authority, contrary to the tenor of the commission under which it is exercised, is void. No legislative act, therefore, contrary to the Constitution, can be valid. To deny this, would be to affirm, that the deputy is greater than his principal; that the servant is above his master; that the representatives of the people are superior to the people themselves; that men acting by virtue of powers, may do not only what their powers do not authorize, but what they forbid.
>
> Until the people have by some solemn and authoritative act, annulled or changed the established form, it is binding upon themselves collectively, as well as individually; and no presumption, or even knowledge, of their sentiments, can warrant their representatives in a departure from it, prior to such an act.

It will be recalled, in considering the methods of enforcing constitutions, that three major means have been developed: popular control, separation of powers, and judicial review. Have any or all of these been included in the Constitution?

As to popular control, the answer is sufficiently obvious—the Constitution imposes, and demands that the government abide by, its terms as the command of the people. But in addition there is set up a system of regular elections for the legislative and executive branches, the objective of which is twofold: first, to provide a popular check on arbitrary or unconstitutional government action; second, within the Constitution, to provide a positive means by which the people can accomplish their political purposes. The elective system, however, is too direct and immediate to satisfy constitutionalists completely. Popular whims and temporary opinions make elections partially ineffective as a means of enforcing obedience to constitutional dictates. This is one further reason for using a written constitutional document: it insulates

---

[2] *The Federalist*, No. 78.

the longer range, more carefully considered political purposes of the people against their own shorter range, less mature desires. The Constitution is an act of the American people of a more basic and enduring nature than laws passed by a representative body. If constitutionalism is limited government, even those who enacted the Constitution must be willing to abide by its provisions unless they wish to go to the extent of amending it.

The separation of powers was an ideal strongly held by the framers of the Constitution. It appears in many of their writings, and is clearly implicit in the provisions of the document. The assumption of the separation of powers is that governments can be kept within bounds by dividing power in such a way that no person or agency possesses enough of it to be dangerous. Three principal items suggest themselves: first, the division of governmental power into three functions, legislative, executive, and judicial, which are to be kept largely independent of each other—an independence, however, that is strongly modified by the addition of checks and balances designed to give each of the three some of the powers of the other two. Second, power was divided further between two legislative chambers, which in the original expectation were to represent two different social classes: the Senate—the upper, propertied groups—and the House of Representatives—the body of the people. Thus it was hoped that the power of the mass would be balanced by the power of property, preventing either from completely dominating the government. Third, power was divided between the state and national governments in the federal system. As has already been remarked, however, no system of separation of powers, working by itself, can guarantee the maintenance of a constitutional system. The basic reason for this appears to be that the balance established is unstable, subject to the shifting tides of economic and political change, and thus temporary. A balance painfully established in 1789 might prove over the years to be woefully inadequate to sustain effective government *or* to maintain constitutionalism.

The third method of enforcing constitutions—judicial review—is the principal subject of this book. Suffice it to summarize here that judicial review has been a part of the Constitution since its inception, even though such is not explicitly stated in the body of the document. No more than separation of powers can judicial review maintain, singlehanded, a constitution. It must be backed by popular self-restraint and by popular belief in the use of judicial review.

It will be seen that the three possible checks on arbitrary power thus boil down to only one in modern democracy: that one is the hold which the constitutional tradition has on the general public. Neither separation of powers nor judicial review is of much use without a public imbued with the idea and ideal of constitutionalism.

The fourth—and most recent—strand of constitutionalism is the use of a written charter. The United States Constitution is such a charter, expressly designed, as we have already seen, as the supreme law of the land, by which all other law is to be judged. The writing of a constitution makes no sense under any other assumption.

One other aspect of constitutionalism may also be discussed in connection with our Constitution. We have seen that English constitutionalism developed a strong distinction between those powers of government which should be relatively unfettered and those rights of the people with which government should not interfere. This distinction is clearly, if implicitly, carried out in our Constitution. The terms of the powers given to Congress are broad and general. The Commerce power, for instance, is conferred on Congress in almost unlimited terms: consequently it has become, under the pressures of the industrial revolution, a vast storehouse of governmental regulatory power. On the other hand, the Bill of Rights provisions state in absolute terms those things which the government shall *not* do; in general, these prohibitions pertain to the individual rights of conscience and speech, rights to fair trial, and (in the Reconstruction Amendments) the right of all to be treated equally by government and the right of all to vote. For the most part these are not economic rights. The Constitution carries on the old British distinction between the powers of government and the rights of the citizenry—a distinction, it may be submitted, that is absolutely necessary to the maintenance of freedom under a strong and effective government.

The Constitution of the United States stands directly in the tradition, and carries out the theory of constitutionalism as we have reviewed it in this chapter. It is one of the results of centuries of search for a method of governing which would provide a rulership that is strong enough to accomplish the tasks set for it by the citizens, and yet can be held to account for its actions and prevented from destroying their freedom. This concept of government is a high one: it demands much in the way of self-discipline of both ordinary citizen and governor, much in the way of wisdom, much in the way of foresight. Many critics believe it demands more than human beings can give. But if such a system can be maintained, it may provide the most secure society possible in a complex and beset world—a government strong enough to *do* and *secure* those things asked of it, yet limited enough so that liberty is also secure.

The Constitution as Tool and as Symbol

Another view of the American Constitution, which fits in well with the foregoing treatment, finds that it is divided into two parts—the *efficient* and the *symbolic*. The efficient parts of the Constitution thus make up a *tool*: they are the power-granting parts, which enable the government to operate effectively. The symbolic parts, on the other hand, make up a statement of limitations expressed as symbolic ideals.

Carrying this theory out, it is said that the principles of federalism, separation of powers, and the Bill of Rights are symbolic, while those of implied powers and enumerated powers are efficient. Often, further, it is claimed that the symbolic portions of the Constitution are so innately vague that they have little practical meaning *except* as symbols —that they cannot be effectively enforced by the courts. If this view were carried to its logical conclusion, it might mean that there could be no judicial review, for symbols would be merely statements of ideals which are nonenforceable: Judge Learned Hand has called them "moral adjurations." But if not carried to this extreme, the idea of a constitution as both tool and symbol becomes a restatement of the principle of constitutionalism as outlined above. A constitution grants power, to be sure, but it also—in the Western tradition—limits the ways in which that power may be rightfully used.

Suggestions for Further Reading

Constitutionalism in the Ancient World

Two excellent works study the ancient concept in some detail: they are Charles H. McIlwain, *Constitutionalism, Ancient and Modern* (Ithaca, N.Y.: Cornell University Press, 1940), and Francis D. Wormuth, *The Origins of Modern Constitutionalism* (New York: Harper & Brothers, 1949). McIlwain's *The Growth of Political Thought in the West* (New York: The Macmillan Co., 1932) is also valuable.

Medieval Constitutionalism

The three works listed above are appropriate here as well. The relevant chapters of George H. Sabine, *A History of Political Theory* (rev. ed.; New York: Henry Holt & Co., 1950) are less technical. For a more detailed and extensive treatment, see R. W. Carlyle and A. J. Carlyle, *A History of Medieval Political Theory in the West* (6 vols · London: Wm. Blackwood & Sons, 1903–36).

The Growth of English Constitutionalism

All the works listed above are relevant. In addition, there are many valuable books, of which only a few are listed here. Perhaps the most accessible and useful for the nonspecialist are John W. Allen, *English Political Thought, 1603–1660* (London: Methuen & Co., 1938); George P. Gooch, *English Democratic Ideas in the Seventeenth Century* (Cambridge: Cambridge University Press, 1927); and Charles H. McIlwain, *The High Court of Parliament* (New Haven: Yale University Press, 1910). The famous work by Sir Frederick Pollock and Frederic W. Maitland, *A History of English Law* (2 vols., 2d ed.;

Cambridge: Cambridge University Press, 1898), is valuable but would be difficult for beginners.

Constitutionalism in the American Colonies

Any good history of the colonial period will give much information on this subject. Special attention may be called to Randolph G. Adams, *Political Ideas of the American Revolution* (Durham, N.C.: Duke University Press, 1922); Edward S. Corwin, *The "Higher Law" Background of American Constitutional Law* (Ithaca, N.Y.: Cornell University Press, 1955); McIlwain, *The American Revolution, A Constitutional Interpretation* (New York: The Macmillan Co., 1923); and Andrew C. McLaughlin, *Foundations of American Constitutionalism* (New York: New York University Press, 1932).

Constitutionalism in the American Constitution

The basic ideas here expounded received their classic statement in Alexander Hamilton's essay, *The Federalist*, No. 78. See also Corwin's work mentioned in the preceding section. There are many other treatments in more general works; see especially Book One of Frank R. Strong, *American Constitutional Law* (Buffalo: Dennis & Co., 1950).

The Constitution as Tool and as Symbol

This conception of the American Constitution was developed by Corwin in a famous article, "The Constitution as Instrument and as Symbol," 30 *Amer. Pol. Sci. Rev.* 1071 (1936). It has been elaborated on in Robert K. Carr, *The Supreme Court and Judicial Review* (New York: Farrar & Rinehart, 1942); and see Beryl H. Levy, *Our Constitution: Tool or Testament?* (New York: Alfred A. Knopf, 1941).

CHAPTER II

Constitutionalism, Modern Democracy, and Judicial Review

> *. . . bear in mind this sacred principle, that though the will of the majority is in all cases to prevail, that will, to be rightful, must be reasonable; that the minority possess their equal rights, which equal laws must protect, and to violate which would be oppression.*
>
> —Thomas Jefferson, *First Inaugural Address*

Constitutionalism was defined in the previous chapter as the concept of limited government. And the fact that the growth of modern democratic governments has complicated the theory and application of constitutionalism was also noted. In addition, the rise of judicial review as a means of enforcing constitutional limitations was briefly discussed, with the conclusion, again, that democracy complicates the picture. Let us now investigate the complications presented by democracy. The author assumes that both constitutionalism and democracy are valid parts of our political heritage; the question to be considered is: Can they coexist?

Constitutionalism and Judicial Review

In the usage of American constitutional law, and as used throughout this book, judicial review will mean *the power of the highest court of a jurisdiction to invalidate, on constitutional grounds, the acts of any other governmental agency within that jurisdiction.* Specifically, this will most often mean the power of the United States Supreme Court to invalidate the actions of any other governmental agency in the United States, whether that agency be state or federal, legislative or judicial.

It will be clear that judicial review is a logical if not the only possible outcome of constitutionalism where there is a written constitution. If a constitution divides powers and prohibits the use of some powers, it is essential that some agency exist which can restrain government from encroaching on those powers withheld. And if a constitution represents a higher law than the ordinary enactments of a legislature—but yet is law—the Anglo-American legal tradition assumes that *as law* it is to be interpreted and applied by courts of law. Law is sometimes defined as those rules of social conduct which will be enforced by government, and the governmental agency most often responsible for such enforcement is the courts. As Chief Justice John Marshall said in a famous case, "It is emphatically the province and duty of the judicial department to say what the law is. Those who apply the rule to particular cases, must of necessity expound and interpret that rule." [1] This has always been a function of American courts. Consequently some of the Founding Fathers and some of our early Supreme Court justices assumed that the Constitution was to be enforced by the Supreme Court, and such has been the practice since the enactment of that document. Only, one would conclude, by amendment (with an extraordinary majority required) can a court decision be overturned.

One other aspect of our belief in judicial review stems from our assumptions about human nature. If it be true that power may be abused, we have most often drawn from the truism the moral that positive power is most dangerous; and the arms of government which possess positive powers are the legislature and the executive. The power of courts, on the other hand, is essentially negative in nature. If this is so, courts are less dangerous to freedom and constitutionalism than the rest of the government, because there is less motive for unjust action, less hope of personal gain. Or to put it differently, courts are more likely to be disinterested. This is, in general, the argument for judicial review stressed by Alexander Hamilton in his famous discussion in *The Federalist*, No. 78. While qualifications are needed before one accepts such arguments fully, there appears to be a good deal of truth in them. The major defect in the argument is the obvious fact that judges, being human beings, are subject to biases and prejudices that prevent them from being disinterested. Even so, it is probable that they are more neutral—because more insulated—than most other governmental officers.

One may add two other significant reasons for the use of judicial review in American constitutional practice. First, ours is a federal system, in which power is divided functionally between the national

---

[1] *Marbury* v. *Madison*, 1 Cranch 137 (1803).

and state governments, and also divided geographically between the various state governments. Conflict and disagreement among these various governments are inevitable. How are such disputes as arise to be settled? There must be some relatively neutral arbiter, and while this would not necessarily have to be a Supreme Court, no other agency was set up by our Constitution to perform the task. Every federal system—unless it is a fictitious one like that of Russia—must have some agency to perform the task of settling disputes; even commentators not essentially favorable to judicial review, such as the Englishman Henry Sidgwick and the Frenchman Alexis de Tocqueville, have conceded as much. That agency in the United States, which judges in terms of the Constitution, is the Supreme Court.

Second, the inclusion of the principle of separation of powers in the Constitution (whatever its wisdom) makes it seem natural that, here too, some relatively disinterested agency exist to moderate conflicts stemming from the rival claims of the executive and the legislature to power. The case for the Supreme Court as the proper arbiter of such conflicts is not as strong as in the case of federalism, for the Court is itself one of the contestants for power. But it is by its nature the weakest of the contestants; and, again, the Constitution provides no other method for settling disputes.

In both the above cases, if there were no agency to settle disagreements, we should long ago have had to create one. Without some umpire such contests would become merely trials of physical strength, eventuating (as one of them did anyway) in civil war, and perhaps in the complete dominance of one branch of the government over the others, and of one government over the others—or, even worse, in the disintegration of the union. These conflicts must be settled in the interest of order; in fact, it may be more important that they be settled peacefully than it is that they be settled constitutionally. But of course the courts work within a constitutional framework; in the end, disputes that cannot be settled judicially by reference to the Constitution are referred to the arena of direct power, where they are settled as may be. Our Civil War is a striking illustration of a conflict over the nature of federalism which could not be settled judicially or constitutionally, but only through trial by arms. The need for judicial settlement of interbranch disputes is illustrated by the conflict over the executive as opposed to the legislative power presented by President Truman's steel seizure order of 1952. The courts have sometimes used the doctrine of political questions to avoid ruling on issues they think are too hot to handle, but the questions must be solved anyway.

Constitutionalism and Democracy

It was pointed out in the first chapter that constitutionalism arose in the predemocratic era of Western history. It was originally evolved in an age of monarchy as an attempt to limit the natural absolutism of that form of government. In England it was transferred fairly easily to the parliamentary oligarchy which controlled British government from the Puritan revolution until the Reform Act of 1832. In America, too, our ideas of constitutionalism stem completely from the colonial and pre-Jacksonian periods, when democracy was but a theory—and a theory not much favored, at that.

The rise of popular government in the mid-nineteenth century presented difficult problems in the reconciliation of constitutionalism with the new ideas of popular sovereignty. In order to put these problems in proper perspective, it is necessary to examine briefly the nature of democracy.

There is little point in attempting to define democracy, for as any student of political thought realizes, it defies precise definition. Nevertheless, the hallmark of democracy appears to be found in the idea that people (nowadays the *whole* people) control the government. While in classical times such an idea always meant *direct* control, in which the people met in a body to make the long-range decisions of government, no modern society has found direct democracy possible. In modern times democracies are indirect, or in the more common terminology, representative. The twin institutions of modern times which are characteristic of democracy, then, are the representative legislature (usually combined with some form of representative executive), and a broad electorate through which the legislature is chosen at fairly regular intervals. It would be too much to say that all countries having these two institutions are democracies; but it is not too much to say that no country without them can be a democracy.

It should be obvious that control by the people, in practice, cannot mean control by all the people, however. All the people seldom if ever agree on anything. For working purposes, all democratic organizations have to assume that the majority can speak and act for all. But this poses a problem, for it means that the majority is making decisions that are disagreeable to the minority—decisions, indeed, that may destroy the political, social, or economic rights and privileges of the minority or of some minority group. The majority, in other words, can be as arbitrary and tyrannical as a single monarch, dictator, or ruling oligarchy. The framers of our Constitution (mostly not "democrats," it must be admitted) saw this, as indicated in the chapter heading quotation from Jefferson and in De Tocqueville's famous phrase "the tyranny of the majority."

Such arguments have often been countered by democrats in more recent times, who point out that few really believe in natural rights any more; and if there are no natural rights, then what rights possessed by a minority could possibly be taken away by the majority? Obviously none. Or, as some other political thinkers believe, politics is nothing but a struggle for power in which God is on the side of the strongest battalions: regardless of right, the strong will get what they want, so why argue about rights? In a democracy the majority is the strongest and consequently has the power to do what it wills.

It is well, however, to look at such arguments rather carefully before accepting them. One need not base an argument for the preservation of minority rights on a natural law basis; one may, in fact, base it on the completely practical grounds that no democracy can long survive as such if it does not allow certain basic rights to its minorities. The operation of popular democracies is, it is true, based on majority rule. But the will of the majority is expressed through the ballot box, and the majority is not always composed of the same people or groups. If Democrats, having a majority, could deprive Republicans of the right to speak or the right to appear on the ballot (as is done in Russia), the practical utility of the elective process would shortly disappear. Merely because a majority has the power to do whatever it wills, the question, What should it will? is not thereby avoided. The very preservation of a democratic system is based on the assumption that the majority will not press for such measures as would destroy the democratic process itself.

An absolute majoritarian democracy, one may then assume, would not long remain a democracy. This fact is given credence not only by logic but by the fact that no absolute democracy has ever long existed. All the modern democracies that have survived for any considerable period have imposed upon themselves certain limitations, either written in constitutions or held by custom and tradition, or both. These limitations, of course, are of the same nature as those heretofore referred to as constitutionalism. Democracies of the modern era are constitutional democracies.

To conclude this analysis, it has by now become obvious that there is no necessary contradiction between democracy and constitutionalism, unless one insists that nothing is democratic if it does not provide unchecked power to the slightest whim of the majority. On the contrary, constitutionalism is the surest means by which the survival of democracy may be ensured. That this depends upon popular belief in the constitutional restraints in no way lessens its significance; indeed, it makes it the more necessary to use every possible means to impress upon the public the need for such restraints. The restraints will, it is true, be most secure when they are so ingrained in custom and tradition that the events of the moment cannot easily shake them—and this is the situation in that most constitutional of all democracies, Great Britain. But lacking this deep, almost instinctive faith in the limitations on its own power, the majority can perhaps be led to observe restraint by the use of logic and persuasion. Especially may this be true when the logic and persuasion are reinforced by a judiciary of immense prestige, speaking in the name of the most revered symbol of American politics, the Constitution.

The Democratic Character of the Constitution

The above argument proceeds on an assumption that has not yet been explicitly stated: that the American Constitution is a democratic document. If popular government requires self-restraint on the part of the body of citizens, the logical conclusion is that the sum of the restraints believed to be required is found in the Constitution.

It would be fallacious, of course, to maintain that our Constitution was in its inception democratic: the facts to the contrary are overwhelming. The framers of the Constitution were not themselves (with a few exceptions) democrats; they did not propose to set up a democracy, but rather a republic based on a rather large propertied class. They were not working within a democratic framework, and probably could not have created a democracy even had they wished to do so. How then can one call the Constitution democratic? In this connection it may be contended that there are two important developments that combine to make it so.

First, even though the Constitution was not originally democratic, *it has been made democratic by later generations.* A document written largely in generalities, it could be fairly easily adapted to democratic purposes without major changes. The essentials of democracy adduced above—a representative legislature and a broad electorate—were both established in principle if not always in fact before the Civil War, and without a single amendment. True, it took the Fifteenth and Nineteenth Amendments to turn theory into fact. But this does not affect the point that the Constitution has been democratized by the American people. We find, therefore, that the Constitution is democratic not because it was intended to be, but because we have made it so in later generations.

Second, *the Constitution has been made democratic by its very acceptance.* This statement does not, of course, refer to the process by which the document was originally ratified by the state conventions. These conventions were not very democratic. What is meant rather is that any constitution that has endured for 170 years and more—over 100 of which were in the essential sense democratic—must be assumed to have "the consent of the governed." No democratic nation (nor perhaps any other) would long submit to being governed constitutionally if it were not disposed to accept the terms of its particular constitution.

These considerations lead to a significant question: If democracy involves rule by majority will, and if the Constitution is regarded as an expression of that will, what happens when the majority later demands things that are not permitted by the Constitution? In order to cope with such a question one must draw a distinction between two types of majority wills: the majority acting as a sober and mature body in its own long-range interest as it sees that interest, and the majority as a day-to-day body shifting in both composition and desire. If a new opinion is strong and permanent enough, it will find its way into the Constitution either by amendment or by some other method.

It will be evident that this book assumes that the United States Constitution represents a mature and relatively stable statement of the political ideals and aspirations of the American people. As such it is democratic in the highest sense of that word, and as such it overrules temporary whims and desires. Should our ideals and aspirations change, there are means available by which to incorporate such changes into the Constitution.

This leaves open the question whether the amending process is properly set up to accomplish its purpose. In order to do so, amendment must be difficult enough to forestall its use as a part of the regular legislative process, but yet easy enough so that major long-range shifts in public opinion can be reflected through it. Without attempting to foreclose the issue, it seems probable that the amending process in the federal Constitution strikes fairly close to the desirable balance.

A major qualification to the above statement is needed. Taken literally it seems to mean that the Supreme Court would have no role to play in the adaptation of the Constitution to new social, political, and economic conditions. It will be recalled that we have earlier alluded to the wise generalities in which much of the Constitution is written. Where specific provisions are involved, it would seem that the role of the Supreme Court must be restricted to enforcing them. If no ex post facto law may be passed, the Court would certainly have the duty and power to invalidate one if it were enacted. On the other hand, where general provisions such as the interstate commerce clause are concerned, the Court shoud be wary of interposing its judgment of constitutionality for that of the legislature. A distinction should also be drawn between the affirmative grants of power, which the courts should properly interpret broadly in order to give the greatest possible opportunity for effective governmental action, and the negative prohibitions on governmental power, which the courts should interpret narrowly in the spirit of constitutionalism. The distinction between affirmative grant and negative prohibition represents our modern restatement of the medieval English line between the legitimate *powers* of government (or prerogative) and the legitimate *rights* of citizens.

If constitutional democracy is to remain both constitutional and democratic, some such theory of the relationships between a constitution and popular government would appear to be necessary.

Democracy and Judicial Review

The great Greek philosopher Aristotle long ago wrote, "To live by the rule of the constitution ought not to be regarded as slavery, but rather as salvation." If the author's analysis of the character of our constitutional democracy is correct, it indicates the truth of Aristotle's statement. The fundamental basis for an enduring democracy is a constitution based on the voluntary self-restraint of the people. The question remains as to how these self-restraints are to work. Are they to be left to chance and the fortunes of political war? To custom and tradition? Or are we to give them the best possible opportunity to assert themselves?

Modern sociology seems to indicate that beliefs are most secure when they are protected by institutions. The institutionalization of an idea provides it with a buffer against the wild and rapid swings which sometimes occur in the public arena. No institution can long preserve liberty in the absence of a strong public sentiment in its favor. But an institution may act as a buffer to blunt the effect of public opinion when it does not represent the settled desires of the public. Some such function may be said to be performed by the Supreme Court in its use of judicial review. No discerning modern student of the Court has claimed that judicial review can prevent public opinion from having its way, or even that it should; but to say that judicial review cannot maintain itself against a strong public opinion is not to say that it is useless. And to say that judicial review may not agree in all respects with the current public opinion is not to say that it is undemocratic, for it may be regarded as democratic in a different sense.

These conclusions may be reached from several avenues of approach. One approach is through the history and theory of constitutionalism, which has already been surveyed. According to this approach, a constitution is an attempt to prevent arbitrary government by imposing limitations on it. But the statement of limitations can mean little unless it has an authoritative interpreter and enforcer. As we have seen, the only even partially effective means of accomplishing this task (in the absence of a very strong tradition) is judicial review. With all its defects, judicial review provides an authoritative and—in our country—popularly accepted means of finding out what the Constitution means. While this cannot be said to guarantee the maintenance of constitutional limitations, by institutionalizing them it certainly gives them a greater strength than they might otherwise possess.

Again, one may approach our conclusions by the way, considered earlier, of an analysis of our Constitution. If the Constitution is in reality a democratic document—made so by usage and acceptance—then one may assume that the institutions set up by the Constitution are also democratized by long acceptance. This is admittedly a "conservative" approach to judicial review: it maintains that judicial review is democratically sanctioned by virtue of the acquiescence of the public in its use over a period of almost 160 years. In this view the fact that judges are not elected and do not directly represent current public opinion is irrelevant: the Supreme Court is democratic not in the representative sense but in the sense that it was created by the will of the people and is performing a function sanctioned by the same will.

This leads to a further point. It may be that in a democracy the power of the people is unlimited; but the citizenry may voluntarily limit the power of the government it sets up through the constitution. A government may be a democratic government, but it is not the people: it merely represents the people. A large part of the argument that judicial review is undemocratic rests on the belief that a democracy must have an unlimited legislature; but this would be so only if the people *wanted* to have a legislature of that nature. The legislatures of the United States, however, have never been regarded as unlimited. They were created, and their powers have always been defined and limited, by constitutional documents theoretically representing the higher and more permanent will of the people. If, then, constitutions are regarded in this light, it is necessary to draw a distinction between the will of the people as expressed in a constitution and that will as expressed in an act of the legislature. If there is a conflict the higher will must rule—unless the constitution itself be changed. The very fact that the Supreme Court is not an elective body makes it more democratic: for it is the one part of our government that is in a practical position to insulate itself against the current (legislative) public opinion as opposed to the more permanent (constitutional) opinion.

In a more strictly American context, it might also be pointed out that history and tradition have imbued the Constitution, the Supreme Court, *and* judicial review with a peculiar sanctity as far as the general public is concerned. This sanctity, it may be argued, has declined somewhat so far as the Court is concerned in recent years, but it is apparently as strong as ever where the Constitution itself is involved. Human beings live at least partially by symbols. It has often been said that the Constitution is one of the symbols by which Americans live. As a result, arguments couched in constitutional terms have great strength. The Supreme Court and its use of judicial review are also symbols of American political ideals. When, therefore, a constitutional argument is buttressed by the Court and the institution of judicial review, its strength becomes even greater.

One may conclude from this that the Supreme Court is not always in a position where it must follow public opinion: the prestige of Constitution and Court are such that in many cases the Court may actually *mold* sentiment. It may even be true that our system of judicially protected rights provides one of the best ways possible by which our political ideals, as expressed in the Constitution, can be held before our people for their emulation. Whether or not it is effective, in this view the Supreme Court was acting in its highest democratic capacity when it declared that the Constitution forbids race segregation in the public schools. Constitution or no Constitution, no other governmental agency in the United States was in a practical position to make such a declaration; nor would it, if made, have had such great effect.

It has sometimes been feared that reliance on a court for the maintenance of constitutionalism involves the danger that the public will lose its own sense of the importance of constitutional principles, thus weakening public responsibility. While not ignoring this possibility, the general line of thought used in this text seems to indicate the contrary. The courts are regarded as a part—and a very important part—of the political process. The discussion of problems and the declaration of principles by the courts become a part of the general flow of ideas and arguments which lead to the formation of public opinion. Thus, as one writer has pointed out, the courts are a "vital element in the community experience through which American policy is made. The Supreme Court is, among other things, an educational body, and the Justices are inevitably teachers in a vital national seminar." Far from weakening the sense of public responsibility, the courts may actually strengthen it, constantly holding before the people the responsibilities that go with democratic self-government.

The general tenor of this viewpoint may be summarized thus:

Government by referendum or town meeting is not the only possible form of democracy. The task of democracy is not to have the people vote directly on every issue, but to assure their ultimate responsibility for the acts of their representatives, elected or appointed. . . . When the judges are carrying out the function of constitutional review, the final responsibility of the people is appropriately guaranteed by the provisions for amending the Constitution itself, and by the benign influence of time, which changes the personnel of the courts. Given the possibility of constitutional amendment, there is nothing undemocratic in having responsible and independent judges act as important constitutional mediators. Within the narrow limits of their capacity to act, their great task is to help maintain a pluralist equilibrium in society.[2]

Before leaving the question of public opinion and its relation to democracy and judicial review, it must be added that, realistically speaking, on most constitutional questions which come to the courts for decision, there is no public opinion. A court or any other agency which attempted to decide such questions by reference to an opinion that did not exist would be in a difficult position. Another difficult question is presented by the fact that there are many publics, and the opinion of one public is likely to be quite different from that of

---

[2] Eugene V. Rostow, "The Democratic Character of Judicial Review," 66 *Harvard Law Rev.* 193 (1952). Copyright 1952 by the Harvard Law Review Association.

another. Which opinion, then, is to govern? These considerations may be illustrated by referring to a specific case or two.

In *Bridges* v. *California*[3] the Court had to decide whether freedom of the press or fair trial was more important in a case in which a newspaper had commented on a trial before its conclusion. It would have been very difficult to discern any public opinion on this matter by which the question could have been decided. Again, in the *School Segregation Cases*[4] there was apparent a vast difference between public opinion in the nation as a whole and the opinion in the South, where segregation is prevalent. If one were to decide on the basis of the public will, which public is to rule? That of the nation or that of the South?

These comments are made merely to illustrate the point stressed above, that modern democracy cannot possibly be "town meeting" democracy. A democratic society is far too large and complex for such procedures. Part of this complexity shows itself in divided public opinion, and in the difficulty of distinguishing any opinion at all in many instances. A complex democratic society requires a complex governmental structure, in which judicial review may well play a very valuable role, both in mediating conflict and in holding the society somewhere near the true course indicated by its political ideals.

Summary

These first two chapters have indicated that American constitutionalism rests on a basis of history, tradition, and logic which provide it with an ongoing prestige in our society. It is nevertheless true that judicial review as an institution has never gone unquestioned; and certainly its use in particular cases has often been challenged. It is also true that, in practice, judicial review forces American courts and judges to play a political role to a far greater extent than has been true elsewhere in the world. It is the task of the rest of this book to elucidate this point and to investigate the actual place the U.S. Supreme Court holds in our political system.

Suggestions for Further Reading

Constitutionalism and Judicial Review

See principally the books of Charles H. McIlwain cited for the previous chapter. The necessity of judicial review in a federal system

---

[3] *Bridges* v. *California*, 314 U.S. 252 (1941).

[4] *Brown* v. *Board of Education*, 347 U.S. 483 (1954), and 349 U.S. 294 (1955).

is discussed by Alexis de Tocqueville, *Democracy in America* (New York: Vintage Books, 1954), Vol. I, Ch. VIII. Also useful are Kenneth C. Cole, "Government, Law and the Separation of Powers," 33 *Amer. Pol. Sci. Rev.* 424 (1939); and Malcolm P. Sharp, "The Classical American Doctrine of the Separation of Powers," 3 *Univ. of Chicago Law Rev.* 385 (1935).

Constitutionalism and Democracy

Again, McIlwain's works are relevant. See also, generally, Carl J. Friedrich, *Constitutional Government and Democracy* (rev. ed.; Boston: Ginn & Co., 1950); Arthur N. Holcombe, *Our More Perfect Union* (Cambridge: Harvard University Press, 1950); Robert M. MacIver, *The Web of Government* (New York: The Macmillan Co., 1948); J. Roland Pennock, *Liberal Democracy: Its Merits and Prospects* (New York: Rinehart & Co., 1950).

Democracy and Judicial Review

There are many general works in the field of constitutional law and constitutional theory which have sections dealing with this question; some are cited immediately above, and many of the works cited in the notes following Chapter VII are worthwhile. Of special interest may be Charles L. Black, *The People and the Court* (New York: The Macmillan Co., 1960). See also Dean Alfange, *The Supreme Court and the National Will* (Garden City: Doubleday, Doran & Co., 1937); Charles A. Beard, *The Supreme Court and the Constitution* (New York: The Macmillan Co., 1912); Edmond Cahn (ed.), *Supreme Court and Supreme Law* (Bloomington: Indiana University Press, 1954); Learned Hand, *The Bill of Rights* (Cambridge: Harvard University Press, 1958); Eugene V. Rostow, "The Democratic Character of Judicial Review," 66 *Harvard Law Rev.* 193 (1952); Carl B. Swisher, *The Supreme Court in Modern Role* (New York: New York University Press, 1958).

CHAPTER III

How the
Supreme Court
Works

> . . . [*T*]*he History of the Supreme Court, as of the Common Law, derives meaning to no small degree from the cumulative details which define the scope of its business, and the forms and methods of performing it.*
>
> . . . [*T*]*he formalities and modes of doing business, which we characterize as procedure, though lacking in dramatic manifestations, may, like the subtle creeping in of the tide, be a powerful force in the dynamic process of government.*
>
> —FELIX FRANKFURTER and JAMES M. LANDIS,
> *The Business of the Supreme Court*

An understanding of the processes and methods by which the Supreme Court accomplishes its tasks is essential to an understanding of American constitutional law. This is true not only because the student would have difficulty figuring out the meaning and importance of much of the Court's work without such knowledge, but because form may often have a powerful effect on substance, as the headnote above indicates. The most basic case in American history—*Marbury* v. *Madison*—cannot possibly be understood without some knowledge of the legal technicalities and processes involved. Issues of jurisdiction, of standing to sue, of whether or not a "case" exists, of exhaustion of remedy—to name only a few—may often determine the result of a case, or even whether it gets a hearing. The Court sometimes is able,

27

in its own discretion, to manipulate these technicalities so as to reach "desirable" results.

Technicalities often seem dull to the student who is not interested in becoming a lawyer; the budding political scientist may question their consequence. Yet, as a famous saying in public administration points out, policy is often "secreted in the interstices" of administrative procedure. No less is it true that much of the policy made by the judiciary, which we are studying in this book, may often be found "secreted in the interstices" of legal procedure.

The Jurisdiction of the Supreme Court

Constitutional and Legislative Aspects of Jurisdiction

The basic question of jurisdiction—that is, what kinds of cases the Supreme Court may handle—is dealt with either expressly or by implication in the Constitution. However, as shall appear, the constitutional provision is skeletal rather than detailed.

The Constitution makes the usual distinction between *original* and *appellate* jurisdiction. Original jurisdiction refers to types of cases which the Court may try in the first instance; appellate, to those which it hears on appeal from other courts. Article III, Section 2, provides that "in all Cases affecting Ambassadors, other public Ministers and Consuls, and those in which a State shall be Party, the supreme Court shall have original Jurisdiction." Although Congress in the Judiciary Act of 1789 attempted to expand this original jurisdiction to include certain other cases, the Supreme Court in *Marbury* v. *Madison*[1] held that the constitutional listing was exclusive, and this attitude has survived to the present day. Original cases arise comparatively rarely, and on the whole are of little importance in the work of the Court.

The appellate jurisdiction of the Court, constitutionally speaking, is somewhat broader, but perhaps the most important aspects of the appellate jurisdiction are drawn by implication rather than by express provision. As a matter of fact, most cases in which judicial review is used fall outside the constitutional definition of the Court's jurisdiction. Two major elements are involved in this expansion: the addition of new appellate jurisdiction by Congressional act and the reception of appeals on constitutional questions from the states.

In the first instance, the appellate jurisdiction granted in the Constitution has not been regarded as exclusive. Congress has made the Supreme Court the final court of appeals for most types of federal cases. Obviously, much of the utility of judicial review would be lost

---

[1] *Marbury* v. *Madison*, 1 Cranch 137 (1803).

if this were not so, for most constitutional cases—so far as federal acts are concerned—arise in the lower courts. It is true, however, that in cases in which the United States government is a party, the Constitution explicitly gives to the Supreme Court appellate jurisdiction, and such cases have constituted an increasing proportion of constitutional issues with the growth of positive government in the United States.

So far as cases from the states are concerned, the Constitution makes no reference to them, except for certain specific categories. But the clause making the Constitution the supreme law of the land has been used by the Supreme Court to justify review as of right in state cases involving the interpretation of the national constitution, treaties, or federal law, and the federal judicial code has always contained provisions for the handling of cases from the state courts.

How Cases Get to the Supreme Court

A mere description of the legal jurisdiction of the Supreme Court does little to clarify the processes by which cases actually reach the Court, so that we must also consider the "flow" of cases and the legal methods involved. For purposes of convenience cases may be divided into two major classes: those that arise in the federal court system, and those that come up from the state courts. They total annually somewhat more than two hundred cases.

With the exception of those few cases in which the Supreme Court has original jurisdiction, a small number that arise directly from district courts, and some cases from the legislative courts, all *federal* cases come to the Supreme Court from one of the eleven courts of appeals. Since the ten circuit courts of appeals are exclusively appellate, it follows that their cases come from lower tribunals such as the United States district courts and the various legislative courts and administrative agencies. Separately, the Supreme Court may receive cases from the Court of Appeals of the District of Columbia, which in turn has received them on appeal from administrative agencies, territorial courts, or the district court for that area.

The second major stream of cases reaching the Supreme Court are those coming from the states. With few exceptions these cases are appealed (or petitions for *certiorari* are applied for) from the highest court of the state. Once in a while a case may bypass the state appeals courts because the state law covering the subject grants no right of appeal, as in *Grovey v. Townsend*, a Negro voting case.[2]

Two Methods Used to Appeal Cases

In most instances there are only two methods for reaching the Supreme Court with a case: these are by *appeal* and by the writ of

---

[2] *Grovey v. Townsend*, 295 U.S. 45 (1935).

certiorari. Appeal to the Supreme Court, like appeals in legal practice generally, is given as a matter of right under well-defined circumstances. Anyone who can plead these circumstances has an affirmative *right* to reach the Supreme Court. However, the circumstances under which appeal is open to a party are severely restricted; also, in recent years the Court has refused to entertain many otherwise legitimate appeals from the states because of "lack of a substantial federal question." Relatively few cases, consequently, reach the Supreme Court by this method. Appeal may be made principally under the following circumstances:

1. When *any* United States court holds an act of Congress unconstitutional in an action to which the United States or its officer is a party, the United States may appeal directly to the Supreme Court.

2. When a circuit court holds a state law unconstitutional or holds that a state law violates a treaty or federal statute, either party may appeal.

3. When a state court has declared a federal statute or treaty unconstitutional, either party may appeal.

4. When a state court *upholds* a state law in a case involving its validity under federal constitution, law, or treaty, either party may appeal.

No other cases may be appealed to the Supreme Court. In recent years about 100 to 125 cases have been heard on appeal each year. If, therefore, a party has no right to appeal a case, and if he cannot secure a writ of certiorari, his final appeal must be to the federal circuit court or to the state court having the final appellate jurisdiction for the particular case.

The writ of certiorari was established by Congress in 1925 in order to enable the Supreme Court to cut down the volume of its work. The theory of the enactment was that most cases can and should be settled without proceeding to the Supreme Court: appeal to a federal circuit court or to a high state court should be enough. The Supreme Court should restrict itself to the fewer but more important cases.

With such purposes it should be clear that certiorari cannot be claimed by the litigant as a right. The litigant *petitions* the Supreme Court for the writ, and the petition is granted or denied at the Court's own discretion. Annually some 1,000 petitions for certiorari are forwarded to the Court; of these, only 120 to 150 are ordinarily granted. Access to the Supreme Court is obviously quite restricted if grounds for appeal do not exist. And the discretionary power of the Court is enhanced, for it alone has the power to decide which petitions will be granted.

The Importance of Appeal and Certiorari

The importance of these methods of reaching the Supreme Court lies in the grounds upon which they may be used. The proper grounds for appeal outlined above are very specific—deliberately so—and express a conscious theory on the part of Congress as to when a party ought to have a *right* to reach the Supreme Court. Two basic ideas appear. In the first place, it is clear that Congress attempted to make it mandatory for the Supreme Court to make the final ruling in *all* cases in which lower courts have found any state or federal law *un*constitutional. Apparently this was mainly to ensure nationwide uniformity in the law, but there also was probably a feeling that the federal courts might not do justice to the states: the Supreme Court was therefore to check all cases of this type. Second, the Court must review on appeal all cases in which a state court has *upheld* state laws against the claim that they violated federal Constitution, law, or treaty. The apparent feeling here was that state courts would be likely to give preference to states as against the federal government, especially since state judges must be elected for limited terms of office.

All of these instances evidence a desire to allow all cases involving the constitutional powers of the federal and state governments to reach the Supreme Court *if* the federal right to act is denied, or if the *state* right to act is denied by a *federal* court.

Certiorari procedure is intended to cover all other important constitutional issues. These are so varied, however, that it is difficult to analyze them. Perhaps the major issues in which certiorari operates are those involving actions by governmental officials as distinct from legislative acts, and those in which a private right is denied in favor of the power of the federal or state government to act. Cases covering situations such as when a convicted person claims he was denied a fair trial; or when a Negro applicant is denied admission to a white law school; or when a public school district sets up a program of religious education—these will almost surely reach the Supreme Court (if at all) by certiorari.

The reasons for which certiorari is granted or denied thus become of great importance. The Court's rule is that all petitions for certiorari are voted upon by the entire membership of the Court; if four or more judges approve the petition, it is granted. On what basis do the judges vote? It seems that the following are ordinarily among the most weighty considerations:

1. How fundamental is the constitutional (or other) issue presented by the case?

2. How many similar cases have been or are being litigated?

3. Is there a conflict of opinion in the lower courts on this particular issue?

4. Does a lower court decision seem to conflict with an earlier Supreme Court decision?

5. Is there a significant individual right involved (as in the habeas corpus cases mentioned below)?

6. Has the lower court departed significantly from the "accepted and usual course of judicial proceedings"?

7. Does the case involve the interpretation of a statute never before construed?

The common denominator in these several reasons is that they all involve important questions of *public* policy: issues that concern not only the litigants in the specific case, but the whole nation. Certiorari procedure consequently has enabled the Supreme Court to become primarily a *public law* court by taking only cases involving public issues; questions involving only private rights are left to the lower courts. The Supreme Court is thus no longer an appellate court in the usual sense, but rather an "adjudicator of issues of public policy in the presentation of which the individual litigant tends to turn into an illustrative figure rather than a principal actor."

The effects of *denial* of certiorari have been the subject of much debate, especially since reasons are never published. It is often assumed that denial means that the Court actually *approves* the lower court decision; but the Court has always maintained that this is not true. Perhaps its view was best stated by the commentator who said that denial of certiorari merely means that the Court "sees no compelling reason to question" the lower court's ruling. But such denial (while it constitutes no precedent, as the Court may later grant certiorari in a similar case) *does* mean that the lower court decision stands, so that as far as the individual litigants are concerned the question whether this constitutes Supreme Court approval is largely academic.

There are various technical reasons for denial of certiorari which, when used, may not affect the constitutional question at all. For instance, Justice Felix Frankfurter has written that the following technical grounds may exist for denial: "Review may be sought too late; the judgment of the lower court may not be final; it may not be the judgment of a State court of last resort; the decision may be supportable as a matter of State Law . . . even though the State court also passed on issues of federal law." It should be recalled, however, that technical though these considerations may be, they can be used by the Court to avoid decision making in cases which for any reason it feels it should not handle.

One other writ has become so important—and somewhat controversial—in recent years that it should be treated briefly here, at least insofar as it affects the work of the Supreme Court. This is the writ of *habeas corpus*. The writ has an ancient and honorable history which cannot be investigated here. For present purposes its chief importance is as a means by which, in combination with the writ of certiorari, an indicted or convicted person may appeal the decision of a state court. One case may serve to illustrate this possibility.

In Tennessee a few years ago an accused man waived his right to counsel on a larceny charge. When he was brought to trial, he found he was also being tried as a habitual criminal. He requested time to obtain a lawyer to defend him against this second charge. The trial court refused this request, and the trial proceeded to his conviction on both counts; the larceny charge carried a three-year sentence, while the habitual criminal charge meant life imprisonment. After serving his prison term on the larceny charge, the prisoner applied to the Tennessee courts for a writ of habeas corpus, asking for his release on grounds that his conviction as a habitual criminal had been in- valid since he had been denied opportunity to obtain counsel. The Tennessee courts refused to issue the writ; the prisoner thereupon petitioned the United States Supreme Court for a writ of certiorari, which was granted. After hearing the case, the Supreme Court ordered Tennessee to issue a writ of habeas corpus, holding that he had been denied due process of law in his trial. Result: He was freed.[3]

Hundreds of such cases have been coming to the Supreme Court in recent times; the decisions on those that are accepted vary, and often certiorari is not granted. The writ of habeas corpus is nonethe- less of great importance, not so much because it affords protection to the individual, significant as such protection is, but because it provides a means by which the Supreme Court may protect the constitutional right to fair trial, and also set up broad standards of what will be regarded as fair trial in the states under the due process clause of the Fourteenth Amendment.

The general importance of certiorari, in addition to its discretionary elements and the fact that it makes the Court primarily a public law court, may be underscored by observing that in recent years over half of the cases that the Supreme Court has decided have come to the Court on writs of certiorari rather than by appeal. The tendency, in fact, seems to be toward more certiorari and less appeal.

The Importance of the Courts of Appeals

An incidental but significant result of the development of certiorari procedures has been, of course, that most federal cases of all types receive their final decision in the circuit courts rather than in the Supreme Court. This is true of almost all strictly private cases, but it is true as well of most cases involving public law issues, for the Supreme Court could not possibly hear fully and decide wisely all such cases. The Supreme Court in recent years has granted only about 10 per cent of all petitions for certiorari. If this proportion applies

---

[3] *Chandler* v. *Fretag*, 348 U.S. 3 (1954).

both to state and federal cases, the result is that the circuit courts must finally decide about 90 per cent of all federal cases that the litigants would like to take to the Supreme Court, and this does not include such cases as the litigants decide not to carry further. It is probably no exaggeration to say that the Supreme Court handles only about 1 per cent of all the cases that reach the circuit courts. This means that even in many important constitutional issues, many questions of statutory interpretation, and many significant administrative law issues, the circuit courts are the courts of last resort. Since they have the same powers of judicial review as the Supreme Court itself, and operate in much the same fashion, most of what is said of the Supreme Court in this and the following chapters is true also of the circuit courts. It would consequently be difficult to exaggerate, and dangerous to ignore, their importance.

Unfortunately, students of constitutional law *have* ordinarily ignored the circuit courts. The consequences of this neglect are that we really know rather little about them, and cannot even assume that our general presumptions about them are correct. We do not know, for instance, whether the circuit courts are on the whole as good as the Supreme Court, whether they are more or less conservative, or whether their judges are more or less "political." Such studies as have been made have indicated that certain circuit courts—either temporarily as the result of having outstanding jurists as judges, or permanently due to uncertain causes—are accorded a great deal more respect by the Supreme Court than others. The Circuit Court of the Second Circuit (New York) for many years has enjoyed such respect, as has the Court of Appeals for the District of Columbia.

The Case or Controversy Rule, Standing to Sue, and Other Rules

In addition to the difficulty encountered in reaching the Supreme Court, which forces most litigants to be satisfied with lower court decisions, let us consider the question of "case or controversy." Associated with this are several other technical questions which may for convenience be lumped under the same heading.

The general legal meaning of a "case or controversy" is that there must be two real parties and a real controversy between them—or, in legal terms, an "adversary interest." This means, at least theoretically, that fictitious, made-up, or "friendly" cases, as well as advisory opinions, are barred. There are difficulties in this theory when it is confronted by court practices, but in a general way it is a regularly observed practice.

The difficulties may be illustrated by reference to a few instances in which the Supreme Court has seemingly ignored the requirement. The stockholder's suit is a well-known example, by which a stockholder sues his company to prevent it from obeying a law that it (the company) does not wish to obey anyway. Then the company as "defendant" defends a cause that is the opposite of its own interest. The *Carter Coal Case* is a famous example.[4] Although the fictitious or collusive elements of such a suit are obvious, many such cases have been received by the Supreme Court. Again, there have been cases in which a company has persuaded an employee (or, as in *Bailey* v. *Drexel Furniture*,[5] the parent of an employee)—probably by paying for the legal costs—to sue it merely to get before the courts, even though the suit might not be in the employee's interest. Still another variant occurred in *Barrows* v. *Jackson*,[6] in which a third party was permitted to bring a damage suit even though the injured party was not involved in the case!

The point of these "exceptions" is merely that the statement of a legal rule, like the wording of a constitution or statute, is always ambiguous enough to permit courts to interpret it, within fairly narrow limits, as they please. Each of the cases mentioned above was one which, at the time, the Supreme Court was apparently eager to decide, and it was thus not disposed to be too strict about the technicalities of the matter. At other times the Court may be very strict, or even too strict.

Another general rule is that of "standing to sue"—a litigant, to be able to reach the courts, must have a personal and substantial interest or injury, differentiated from that of the general mass of citizens. Thus, taxpayers suing *as* taxpayers are often refused access to the courts because their "pocketbook injury" is no greater than that of any other citizen.[7]

Two other questions are of some importance. The courts often will ask whether an injury is *real* or merely *hypothetical*. That is, has the plaintiff *been* injured or does he merely feel he *will be* injured? Like the other considerations adduced above, this one is often ignored. For instance, in most of the rate cases which were so common while substantive due process was in vogue—*Smyth* v. *Ames*[8] may serve as an example—the courts were really involved in a game of prediction. For the company in such cases was complaining that the rate set by the state would not (in the future) permit it to earn a fair return. And the court had the job of predicting what rate of return would result from a particular rate structure. There was, then, no present injury nor even any assurance (in advance of the court's determination) that there would be an injury. Also, in the *Pierce Case*[9]

---

[4] *Carter* v. *Carter Coal Co.*, 298 U.S. 238 (1936).
[5] *Bailey* v. *Drexel Furniture Co.*, 259 U.S. 20 (1922).
[6] *Barrows* v. *Jackson*, 346 U.S. 249 (1953).
[7] See *Massachusetts* v. *Mellon*, 262 U.S. 447 (1923), and *Doremus* v. *Board of Education*, 342 U.S. 429 (1952).
[8] *Smyth* v. *Ames*, 171 U.S. 361 (1898).
[9] *Pierce* v. *Society of Sisters*, 268 U.S. 510 (1925).

the courts enjoined the enforcement of an Oregon act requiring all children to attend public schools before it even became operative.

Yet if the courts for some reason do not wish to rule on a question, this rule, like the others, is a convenient one to use. It was used to preclude ruling on the cases of federal employees who had not violated the Hatch Act (which was intended to prevent political influence in the civil service) but wished to secure an injunction against its enforcement so that they could engage in political activity.[10] The Court held, in substance, that the only way they could get to court was to violate the law first, be discharged from their jobs, and then go to court. And in *International Longshoreman's Union* v. *Boyd*,[11] alien cannery workers who went to Alaska (then a federal territory) each summer for the canning season applied for relief from the McCarran Immigration Act, which might have worked so as to prevent them from getting back into the United States after the season; the Court used the same idea to avoid ruling. Consequently a worker would apparently have to take the chance of being excluded. Justices Black and Douglas have dissented in such cases, believing that the Federal Declaratory Judgment Act was intended to allow the courts to use "a wise discretion" in accepting them. Douglas pointed out, in regard to the public workers, that to require these employees first to suffer the hardship of a discharge is not only to make them incur a penalty, but it makes inadequate, if not wholly illusory, any legal remedy which they may have. The equity doctrine of "threatened irreparable injury" would seem to be in point here.

Even an *actual* injury may not always be enough, for the damage must be a "legally reparable" one. This is a rule that is particularly applicable to administrative law cases although not confined to them. In a 1939 TVA case, the Tennessee Electric Power Company and seventeen others were denied standing to sue because of a competitive injury from TVA; competition, said the Court, was not enough to give standing, no matter how injurious it might be.[12]

It is thus obvious that the courts have a good deal of discretion in applying the rules of standing to sue and of case or controversy. On the whole this is probably just as well, even though there are many critics of the way this discretion is used. One may find the following benefits flowing from a fairly rigid insistence on the procedures outlined above:

[It assures] that constitutional issues of great importance will be raised with adversary parties—and with the court thus deriving the benefit of more or less well-briefed, well-pleaded, and well-argued cases.

---

[10] In *United Public Workers* v. *Mitchell*, 330 U.S. 75 (1947).

[11] *International Longshoreman's Union* v. *Boyd*, 347 U.S. 222 (1954).

[12] *Tennessee Electric Power Co.* v. *Tennessee Valley Authority*, 306 U.S. 118 (1939).

[It relieves the defendant] of the cost and trouble of defending in an action where the plaintiff has no substantial personal interest in the outcome of the suit; frivolous actions are thus discouraged.[18]

Further, it relieves the Supreme Court of part of an overwhelming burden, by cutting down the number of cases which it must consider.

On the other hand, those who hope for a relaxation of the rules—particularly in civil rights cases—point out that rigid application may make it difficult to get a ruling on even an important law. It may be hard for anyone to prove a personal and substantial interest differentiated from that of the citizenry, or an actual injury. Justice Frankfurter's opinions in the *Longshoreman's Union* and several other cases seem to indicate a deliberate intent to avoid ruling on constitutional issues wherever possible. The trouble is, however, that this approach may have the effect of condoning or even encouraging government action interfering with civil rights, and may even make it more difficult to reach court when the injury becomes more general. In some cases if a taxpayer's interest is not enough, for instance, it is hard to see how a law could be challenged. This has been publicly debated during the 1961 controversy over federal aid to parochial schools. Perhaps a doctrine of "class" interests could be used to take care of such situations.

It seems unjust, further, to force a person to violate a law and suffer the consequences of violation in order to test its validity. This is especially true when the penalty is as severe as exclusion from the country or loss of employment.

In addition to the elements of a case and of standing to sue, two other factors in reaching the Supreme Court should be mentioned. One is the doctrine of exhaustion of remedy. This is particularly applicable to cases from the states and from administrative agencies. The doctrine, in substance, is that appeals or certiorari will not be granted unless all the legal steps available at lower levels have been taken. For instance, ordinarily cases may not be appealed to the United States Supreme Court directly from a state trial court. The only exception would occur if the state made no provision for any appeal to a higher state court. The reason for this doctrine is rather plain: the states and administrative agencies should be given every possible opportunity to provide justice, and the Supreme Court should not be burdened with cases where that opportunity has not been given.

An associated rule is that the Supreme Court will not interpret a state law in advance of an interpretation by the highest relevant state authority. For instance, the Court refused to rule on the validity of the Michigan loyalty oath in 1953, reasoning that the Michigan

---

[18] Ernest R. Bartley, unpublished paper presented before the American Political Science Association, September, 1956.

Supreme Court had not yet construed the statute.[14] The theory is that the state court may interpret the law in such a way as to avert any constitutional issue, thus making it unnecessary to resort to the Supreme Court.

The accent of these rules, like most of those surveyed earlier, is the twofold aim of preserving an orderly legal process and conserving the energies of the Supreme Court, while yet serving the cause of maintaining and providing justice for litigants.

The Doctrine of Political Questions

The doctrine of political questions is, as the name implies, an admission by the courts that a particular question can or should be answered by the "political" agencies of government rather than by judicial decision. The doctrine originated in Chief Justice Roger B. Taney's opinion for the Supreme Court in *Luther v. Borden*. This case arose out of the circumstances of Dorr's Rebellion in Rhode Island in 1842. Dissatisfaction with the state's archaic constitution had led to a dissident group's attempt to set itself up as the government of the state under a new constitution, and the Court was asked to determine which was the legal government. In refusing to rule on the question, Taney said:

. . . [While the Supreme Court] should always be ready to meet any question confided to it by the Constitution, it is equally its duty not to pass beyond its appropriate sphere of action, and to take care not to involve itself in discussions which properly belong to other forums. No one, we believe, has ever doubted the proposition, that, according to the institutions of this country, the sovereignty in every State resides in the people of the State, and that they may alter and change their form of government at their pleasure. But whether they have changed it or not, by abolishing an old government, and establishing a new one in its place, is a question to be settled by the political power. And when that power has decided, the courts are bound to take notice of its decision, and to follow it.[15]

The doctrine of political questions, it should be noted, is a doctrine of discretion and self-restraint. Only the Court can decide when to use it. It will hardly be argued that the Court's choices as to when to use and when not to use the doctrine have always been wise. But it is probable that in many cases its use has kept the Court out of embarrassing situations in which its decisions might not be enforceable even if made.

The constitutional logic of the doctrine is dubious even if its political wisdom is certain. It should be clear to all readers of this book that it is impossible to categorize cases into those which are "political"

---

[14] *Albertson* v. *Millard*, 345 U.S. 242 (1953).
[15] *Luther* v. *Borden*, 7 Howard 1 (1849).

and those which are not. Constitutional cases are by their very nature political. They all involve deciding questions which *could* be decided by other governmental agencies. Consequently, the doctrine of political questions, far from expressing a judgment that the courts *should not* rule on a particular type of question, in reality constitutes an admission that they *cannot*. In other words, the courts must make the difficult and sophisticated judgment as to whether a decision in a particular case will be acceptable and enforceable. Such a judgment demands the highest type of political acumen and judicial statesmanship. It emphasizes once more the large elements of discretion which courts possess.

The Case in Court

Once a case has reached the Supreme Court, what happens to it? How does the Court consider cases? How does it dispose of them? What are its working methods? These questions are both interesting and important. They may affect not only the disposition of the individual case, but the effect it will have on public opinion, legal opinion, and future cases involving similar questions.

Courtroom Procedure

The Supreme Court is in session from the first Monday each October until early in June. This is known as the "October Term, 1962" for the term beginning in October of that year. The Court convenes at ten each day, goes to lunch from twelve to twelve thirty, and recesses for the day at two thirty. Early mornings and the evenings are normally spent in study of cases. Cases are heard Monday through Thursday at present, with the judicial conference (discussed a little later) scheduled for Friday. This means that with oral argument limited to two hours per case, the Court may be expected to handle about eight full cases in a week. After two weeks, in which fifteen to twenty cases may have been heard, the Court usually recesses for another two weeks in order to allow the judges time to study the written briefs, prepare opinions, and carry out their other duties. About three Mondays a month are set aside as "opinion days," when decisions are announced and the opinions accompanying them are read.

The Court meets in a marble palace across a green from the Capitol; the building itself is cold but impressive as befits the nation's highest court. In the building are various offices for the employees of the Court; a public cafeteria; a suite of offices for each justice, his law clerk and secretary; a library; a conference room; and, of course, the courtroom. The courtroom is rather small, seating only about three hundred people. Although it now contains a public address system, complaints are still heard that the poor acoustics make it impossible for many spectators to hear what is going on.

This impressively dignified, red velure-draped room is the scene of equally dignified ceremony: the judges appear, like actors, from behind the drapes; the Chief Justice parts the curtain behind the bench, takes his place behind his chair, and is followed seriatim by the associate justices in order of seniority. They remain standing until the marshal has completed his introduction:

> Oyez, Oyez, Oyez! All persons having business before the Honorable, the Supreme Court of the United States are admonished to draw near and give their attention, for the Court is now sitting. God save the United States and this Honorable Court.

But while the room and the ceremony are austere, the justices themselves, though normally men of mature dignity, are nevertheless human and often act like human beings. In the *Income Tax Case* in 1895, Justice John Marshall Harlan delivered a powerful dissenting opinion during which he apparently got so worked up that he shook his finger under Justice Stephen J. Field's nose (Field had written a strong concurring opinion). His dissent was so strong that Attorney General Philander C. Knox said, "I should hate to use any such language about the Court as it said about itself yesterday." Field, for his part, probably contributed to Harlan's intemperance, for he showed his distaste for Harlan's opinion by loudly rustling papers and whispering. One wonders what had transpired in the judicial conference on that case! [16]

In the days before the Court's load grew so heavy, oral argument was the principal method of presenting a case. Argument was unlimited in time; such lawyers as Daniel Webster would take days in presenting a case, and Justice Joseph Story called this long-windedness "excessively prolix and tedious." But now argument is limited to one hour for each side, including the time taken by the justices in interposing questions. Consequently, the written brief has replaced oral argument as the more important factor in the presentation of a case. The remaining importance of oral argument probably is the opportunity it gives to the justices to question attorneys on particular points which may not be covered satisfactorily in the briefs.

It should perhaps also be noted that in appellate practice as distinct from the trial courts, there are no witnesses, no jury, no cross-examination, or any of the features that appear in movie versions of great trials. There are a few hundred spectators (most of whom do not really know what is going on), the lawyers for each side (the parties themselves are seldom present, and never officially), the justices, and various court officers. All that happens is the reading of the arguments

---

[16] *Pollock v. Farmers' Loan and Trust Co.*, 158 U.S. 601 (1895).

plus some interspersed questions from one judge or another. The procedure is normally quiet and decorous; dramatic pleas to the jury are notable by their absence. Even here, however, lawyers have at times verged on the tearful in presenting cases to the Court. George Wharton Pepper is famous for his argument in the *AAA Case*,[17] which involved federal relief to farmers during the New Deal. After delivering a long eulogy to the virtues of private property, he concluded:

. . . But I do not want your Honors to think that my feelings are not involved, and that my emotions are not deeply stirred. Indeed, may it please your Honors, I believe I am standing here today to plead the cause of the America I have loved; and I pray Almighty God that not in my time may "the land of the regimented" be accepted as a worthy substitute for "the land of the free."

The Friday Conference

For many years the Supreme Court worked on a six-day week, holding its judicial conference on Saturday, when, as Justice Harlan F. Stone remarked, "the call for golf is most alluring." Chief Justice Earl Warren and his colleagues may have found the call for golf too alluring, for in 1953 they changed the conference to Friday, announcing at the time that they expected to be able to handle as many cases as previously even on a five-day week.

The conference has as its purpose the discussion of the cases and other matters before the Court. Normally it will cover those cases argued in the days preceding the conference. The justices are expected by Friday to have read the voluminous briefs and other data, and to be able to come to conference with some idea of a proper decision. Justice Stone continued his discussion of the conference in these words:

. . . [E]ach case is presented for discussion by the Chief Justice, usually by a brief statement of the facts, the questions of law involved and with such suggestions for their disposition as he may think appropriate. . . . Each judge is prepared to discuss the case at length and to give his views as to the proper solution of the questions presented. . . . Each judge is requested by the Chief Justice, in the order of seniority, to give his views and the conclusions which he has reached. The discussion is of the freest character and at its end, after full opportunity has been given for each member of the Court to be heard and for the asking and answering of questions, the vote is taken and recorded in the reverse order of the discussion, the youngest, in point of service, voting first.[18]

It is in conference that the mettle of a justice is tested, for here he must meet his colleagues in the rough and tumble of free discussion.

---

[17] *United States v. Butler*, 297 U.S. 1 (1936).
[18] Harlan Fiske Stone, "Fifty Years' Work of the U.S. Supreme Court," 53 *American Bar Assoc. Journal* 259 (1928).

Out of this discussion, it is expected, some consensus will emerge to which at least a majority of the Court may adhere, and which can be embodied in the opinion of the Court.

The Decision

With rare exceptions, every case has a winner and a loser. The *decision* makes this choice. It is, for the individual parties to each case, the most important thing about the case; it may mean life or death, or millions of dollars. And from the standpoint of the maintenance of a system of justice, the "justice" of the whole depends on the justice of the individual cases which make up the whole.

Nevertheless, from the standpoint of constitutional law the decision is of importance not because of its disposition of the cases of the litigants as such, but because of the wider application and the principle involved; in other words, the public policy enunciated by the decision is more important to the student of constitutional law than what happens to the litigants. Then too, the importance of each decision must be assessed from two other viewpoints: what it means for similar cases which may arise in the future, and what it means for the whole body of constitutional powers and limitations and the maintenance of constitutional government. As noted previously, the individual litigants are turned into symbolic representatives of a cause, and the decision, important as it is to them, is more significant because of its wide ramifications in the social, economic, and political realms.

From the technical standpoint, little needs to be said about the decision, though decisions are often legally quite complex. The Supreme Court's decisions consist basically of orders to someone to do or not to do something. Decisions are reached, as pointed out above, by vote of the members of the Court (of the nine members or of some smaller number if there is a vacancy, illness, a new justice who has not heard the case, or a voluntary disqualification of himself by a justice who feels he cannot ethically participate in a particular case because of personal interest in its outcome). The Court works on a straight majority principle. Several complications arise in rather rare instances. For example, if one judge is not participating, a tie vote is possible. When this happens two alternatives are open to the Court: to decide the case anyway (which has the practical effect of upholding the decision of the next lower court), or to postpone decision until the absent member returns. Officially the second alternative is rarely used, but since the Court itself decides *when* to issue decisions no outsider can tell how often it is used unofficially.

Again, it sometimes happens that there are more than two possible ways of disposing of a case, so that perhaps there is no majority approving any possible disposition. In this difficult circumstance the

Court has rendered itself powerless through its own inability to find a majority solution, and again the decision of the next lower court must be allowed to stand.

It should be noted, however, that in both of the above situations the major *issue* of the case (as distinct from the litigants) has not been settled at the highest level. Consequently it may seem worthwhile to lawyers to present the Court at some future date with a similar case in the hope that it will then be able to decide, due to new personnel or other changes.

Finally, it is important to know that the decision of the Supreme Court does not necessarily finish litigation in a case. It may merely decide a particular point of law, leaving it to the lower courts to re-judge the same case in the light of the Supreme Court decision of the legal point. After the lower court has done this, the case may find its way to the Supreme Court again because of some other question. Thus, when Virgil Hawkins, a Negro, was denied admission to the University of Florida Law School, he appealed to the Supreme Court, which remanded the case to the Florida Supreme Court for rehearing "in the light of" the *School Segregation* decision. The Florida Supreme Court stalled by appointing a commissioner to study whether Hawkins could safely be admitted to the university; but Hawkins appealed again to the Supreme Court, which then vacated its previous judgment and ordered him admitted. The ups and downs of this one case took over seven years, and Hawkins was never actually admitted to the university.[19]

The Opinion of the Court

The fact that normally opinions accompany decisions has already been mentioned. This is typical of Anglo-American legal systems, and the use of written opinions goes far back in English history. The usefulness of opinions should be fairly clear. In a case-and-precedent legal system like ours, the bare decision is almost meaningless, since seldom are two cases exactly alike. It would be difficult, therefore, for lawyers to interpret decisions and make any intelligent judgment of their applicability to succeeding cases if it were not for the written opinion.

From the standpoint of constitutional law, moreover, the written opinion takes on added importance. If a constitutional decision is a settlement of an important policy question, it is important to know just what policy question has been settled, and how; but the decision itself gives only a clue to these matters. It remains for the opinion to clarify and generalize. The opinion, in other words, puts flesh on

---

[19] *Florida* ex rel. *Hawkins* v. *Board of Control,* 347 U.S. 971 (1954), 350 U.S. 464 (1956), 355 U.S. 839 (1957).

the bare bones of the decision. Lawyers, government officials, and the general public can use the opinion as a basis for action.

Then, too, the writing of opinions is an aid in preventing judges from giving too much weight to their own preconceptions and biases. The fact that they must state their reasons for all to see, that the statement is open to criticism and later reversal, effectively forces the individual judge to rationalize his case in terms of American constitutionalism. If his reasoning is faulty someone is sure to find the faults and return to the attack in future cases, thus affecting the course of future interpretation. If his reasoning, on the other hand, is powerful it may withstand the buffeting of centuries of social and economic change. Lord Coke, a seventeenth-century English judge, is still quoted today by American jurists.

The opinion of the Court, then, may be said to have a twofold purpose: to explain the reasons why the decision was made as it was, and to point the way for courts, lawyers, government, and public when other similar situations arise. It incidentally serves a third but very significant purpose—that of putting judges on their good behavior. Walton Hamilton has summarized the values of a written opinion by pointing out that it "serves the multiple purpose of helping the bench to be critical of its own intellectual processes, keeping lower courts in order, announcing legal standards for acceptable human conduct, extending the courtesy of an answer to arguments which do not prevail and affording an opportunity to justify an argument."

Usually the opinion of the Court is a majority opinion, and laymen sometimes loosely so refer to it. In other words, if five or more judges vote to decide a case a certain way, they will ordinarily be able also to get together on the reasons for their votes. The opinion of the Court attempts to state reasons for decision on which all the members of the majority can agree; it is thus to a rather significant degree an institutional opinion, even though it is actually written by an individual. The individual gives it his own peculiar literary style and his own method of organizing and stating the reasoning, but the actual reasons are those that gain the support of his colleagues. This is why it is difficult to tell exactly how much of Marshall's great opinions expressed his own convictions: he may have had to compromise at times in order to gain a majority. The same is true of all opinions agreed to by a majority of the Court. The individual may add strength to the opinion by the power of his logic, or he may weaken it; but the basic reasoning is not his alone but that of at least four other men. This institutionalizing of the opinion has both good and bad effects on its strength. On the one hand, it forces the court to rely only on those reasons that a majority can support—a factor that makes for a greater legal and popular support. But at the same time the very fact that it *does* need majority support is likely to cause it to be watered down, sometimes to the point of being innocuous.

The opinion is written by a judge to whom it is assigned by the senior member of the majority, or by the Chief Justice in the more usual cases in which he stands with the majority. Most judges have certain types of cases in which they are specialists, and such cases will normally be given to them for opinion writing, subject to the natural obligation of keeping the workload fairly apportioned among all the judges. Often the Chief Justice will assume the sometimes distasteful burden of writing the opinions in the more controversial cases.

Now and then a case will arise in which, even though five or more justices will agree as to the decision, no line of reasoning can be found which a majority can accept. In such instances the opinion of the Court may not exist at all; only the decision can be said to be "by the Court." Generally, in such cases, the "opinion of the Court" will in fact be not an opinion at all but merely a statement of the facts of the case and the decision, and all the actual opinions will have the status of concurring opinions. In the important *Steel Seizure Case* of 1952, Justice Hugo Black's opinion for the Court was extremely brief: probably because he could say little on which the six-judge majority could agree. There were five other opinions by the majority! [20]

Frequently in cases that follow rather strictly a precedent, or for various other reasons, the Court will not feel it necessary to write a full opinion. At such times a *per curiam* (literally, "by the Court" as a whole) opinion may be used; it is a statement of the decision and of the precedents on which it is based, often no more than a short paragraph long. Both of the *Hawkins* opinions discussed above were *per curiam*. It is usually but not necessarily true that *per curiam* opinions are not used unless the Court is unanimous.

Writing an Opinion

There is some doubt, keeping the above considerations in mind, as to the value or wisdom of literary style in a judicial opinion. Some judges, indeed, have striven consciously to avoid such style, seeking instead merely to say in plain and simple language what is intended. The biographer of Hughes gives that Chief Justice's beliefs as follows:

The qualities that he sought to infuse into his opinions were accuracy, clarity, conciseness, and power. These were the four corners of good judicial craftsmanship. It was not the function of the judge to write literature. The struggle for catch phrases, rhetorical flourishes, and stylistic effects too often

---

[20] *Youngstown Sheet & Tube Co. v. Sawyer*, 343 U.S. 579 (1952).

led to obscurities and equivocal statements. . . . The test of a good opinion was not whether it beguiled the public but whether it made the court's judgment unmistakably plain to the lower courts and the bar.[21]

Hughes's ideas are certainly understandable and on the whole praiseworthy. At the same time they are legalistic and seemingly unaware that court decisions have other than legal effects. The impact of an opinion cannot be confined to the bench and bar; and some of the opinions that live in history have been those written with a sense of literary style or with style governed not by legal craftsmanship but by strong emotion. Used with care, it may be added, imagery is not necessarily imprecise. A judge should, no doubt, be careful not to become so wrapped up in his style that his words become meaningless; but it does no harm if he combines with this care a knowledge that he is writing for posterity and politics as well as for lawyers. There is room in opinion writing for the Holmesian phrase as well as the Hughesian precision.

Judges inevitably fall at times into the snare of saying more than they need to say in an opinion. Statements of opinion or interpretation that are not necessary to the course of reasoning of an opinion are known as *obiter dicta*—judicial "asides." Such statements are important in constitutional law, however, because they provide clues as to what the judge had in mind and give some basis on which future actions may be predicted. The judicial ideal is to confine the reasoning of an opinion to the precise set of facts confronting the Court in the individual case; but as with most ideals, it is seldom achieved. There is even some doubt from the public policy standpoint whether it should be an ideal. For one of the principal values of an opinion is the knowledge that it will apply to other cases which are not exactly the same. If the Court's reasoning is too narrowly confined to the case in hand, no one can easily predict how the decision *does* apply to other cases; and the consequent doubt leads to later litigation which might have been avoided if the Court's reasoning had been somewhat broader.

Obiter dicta may sometimes also provide judges with an opportunity for giving subtle hints to lawyers as to how they could approach the Court with better chances of success. For the lawyer's arguments and claims usually are regarded as confining the Court; it is usually thought improper for the Court to introduce legal points not brought up by the parties. But a judge may remark in passing that if such a question *had* been raised it might have made a difference in the decision, thus extending an open invitation to the litigant to try again. Of course, the use of doctrines such as "affectation with a public interest" or "clear and present danger" provide the same sort of clues to lawyers.

---

[21] Merlo J. Pusey, *Charles Evans Hughes* (New York: The Macmillan Co., 1951), Vol. II, p. 679.

Concurring and Dissenting Opinions

If a judge agrees with the Court's decision but not with the reasons given in the opinion of the Court, he may write a separate opinion in which he gives his own reasons for reaching the same conclusion. Such opinions are known as concurring opinions—they say "I concur in the result but not in the reasoning by which it was reached." In the Steel Seizure Case[22] there were five concurring opinions; in the Texas Jaybird Case[23] there was an 8–1 decision but no opinion supported by a majority at all—Black's opinion gained the support of only two others, Clark's of three others, while Frankfurter stood by himself.

The concurring opinion has two important effects: it weakens the influence of the decision by indicating splits within the majority; and it opens the way to further litigation on similar questions by introducing doubt as to the real meaning of the decision. It also makes it difficult to use the case as a precedent if there is no majority opinion at all. While concurrences have become increasingly common in Supreme Court practice, they seem on the whole unjustifiable. True, in cases of serious difference, it may be better to have the various views expressed than not. But many concurring opinions seem to have been formulated only to satisfy the ego of the writer; they often concern minor differences or legal technicalities, and some of them seem written for the primary purpose of showing off the literary style of the justice. It seems likely that somewhat more restraint in the use of the concurring opinion would be a good thing. Possibly the courts could adopt the device used in the Report of the Commission on Intergovernmental Relations, of having disagreement with particular portions of the majority opinion expressed in brief footnotes rather than in separate statements. This would have the effect of emphasizing the over-all agreements instead of the specific differences.

The dissenting opinion, on the other hand, seems to be a necessary and desirable part of appellate court practices. If a judge cannot bring himself in conscience to accept the majority decision, he has not only the right but the duty to give his reasons. From the standpoint of policy, the legal and lay publics have a right to his opinions. If courts had proven infallible or if they were merely legal slot machines, there would be no purpose in dissent. But since our court system imposes on the judges the difficult task of settling important policy questions by reference to a document notable for its ambiguity, there is a real place and function for the dissent. Chief Justice Hughes called the dissent "an appeal to the brooding spirit of the law, to the conscience of a future day." It provides an argument opposing that of the majority which may be seized on by lawyers and urged in

---

[22] See note 20, this chapter.
[23] Terry v. Adams, 345 U.S. 461 (1953).

succeeding cases with some hope of success. It calls attention to defects in the position of the majority, forcing rethinking and perhaps strengthening of that position. Further, it calls the majority to the bar of public opinion and of enlightened legal opinion. As Justice Henry Billings Brown once pointed out:

> It is urged upon one hand that dissents inevitably weaken the authority of the court. This as an immediate effect is doubtless true, but in the passage of years it often happens that the authority of the court is strengthened by the failure of a dissent to impress itself upon the final judgments of the public.
>
> If the authority of the court is weakened by a dissent, it is probably because it ought to be weakened.

It is sometimes said that unanimous opinions have a special force and prestige because of their unanimity. But this can only be true where there is the possibility of dissent. Unanimity gains its force from its voluntary nature. Therefore one might say that without dissenting opinions all court decisions would be on the same level—an undifferentiated mass.

This is not, however, the same thing as saying that every dissenting opinion ever written should have been written. Some, no doubt, have been based upon captious or insignificant reasons and might better never have seen the light. And in addition, there has been, especially in recent years, a tendency for each dissenting judge to write his own opinion—a practice which partially destroys the force of dissent by depriving it of any focus, and which emphasizes the unwillingness of the judges to compromise even on relatively minor points.

One of the major criticisms of the Court in recent times has been that each judge seems to insist on expressing himself as an individual even though he may have nothing significantly different to say. To the extent that this is true the Court would probably benefit from the exercise of greater self-restraint by its members both as to the concurring and the dissenting opinion.

It might be noted here that some of our greatest judges have made their reputations primarily in dissent. This is true of Justices William Johnson, John Marshall Harlan, Oliver Wendell Holmes, Louis D. Brandeis, William O. Douglas, and Hugo Black—all of the Supreme Court. It is true also of Judge Henry Edgerton of the Court of Appeals of the District of Columbia and Judge Michael Musmanno of the Pennsylvania Supreme Court. Dissents have been of practical importance in providing a standard to which later generations can turn. It is astonishing to note, for instance, the large number of the first Justice Harlan's dissents which have later in one way or another found their way into the law. It might almost be said that Harlan was a more significant judge in dissent than most of his contemporaries were in majority.

Precedent and Reversal

In disposing of a case an appellate court usually has two basic alternatives: to follow, or not to follow, precedent cases. The exception is the case that is so unprecedented as to have no precedents. In general, lower courts are required to follow the precedents set by higher courts, whereas the highest court is free to do as it pleases in this respect. But to state the case thus simply is to ignore the lawyer-like resourcefulness of judges. They have found at least three other alternatives to obscure what they are doing.

There are, then, five things that a court may do in regard to precedent. Most obviously, it may follow (or "affirm") the precedent —and in most periods of history, usually does. For the stability of any legal system depends to a large extent on its predictability, so that citizens can reasonably be expected to know what is legal. This is what Justice Owen J. Roberts had in mind when, after a string of reversals by the Court, he dissented, and charged that it is "the present policy of the court freely to disregard and to overrule considered decisions and the rules of law announced in them," a practice which, he said, "tends to bring adjudications of this tribunal into the same class as a restricted railroad ticket, good for this day and train only."

On the other hand, a legal system that was completely certain would be one that was completely inflexible. A rigid adherence to precedent would prevent the law from easily changing to meet new conditions. When the law to be interpreted is, like the Constitution, rather difficult to change formally, and ambiguous and difficult to interpret to begin with, the overruling of precedent is sometimes the wise policy.

A second course with regard to precedent, thus, is just as obvious: to reverse it. This is known as "overruling." A simple matter technically, reversal of precedent has important implications constitutionally. For it means that the Court is changing its interpretation of the Constitution, a change that is significant far beyond its effect in the case before it. When the Court, for instance, specifically overruled the *Child Labor Case*[24] in *United States* v. *Darby*,[25] it meant a whole new method of approaching the commerce clause, and thereby made it possible for Congress to pass many laws that would previously have been constitutionally suspect. Overruling is, then, one of the methods by which the Court can adapt the Constitution to new times and new circumstances. It is used most often in transitional, fast-changing periods in our history; "as conditions and opinion become stable, the law tends toward organic unity; at the impact of an advancing culture it becomes disorderly."

[24] *Hammer* v. *Dagenhart*, 247 U.S. 251 (1918).
[25] *United States* v. *Darby Lumber Corp.*, 312 U.S. 100 (1941).

Third, considering the number of cases that have flowed through the Anglo-American court systems, it is quite often possible to choose between two or more different lines of precedents; or even more likely, to choose between different interpretations of the same precedents. Thus a decision may be reached which, without formally disturbing precedents, may yet start the courts off on a new tangent. In the *Income Tax Case*,[26] for instance, the majority and minority read entirely different meanings into the major precedent case, *Hylton* v. *United States*.[27]

A fourth way of treating precedents is merely to ignore their existence. This is done in order to express certain attitudes; perhaps the Court thinks the precedents are largely irrelevant or unimportant. Or perhaps, for policy reasons, it does not wish to overrule the precedent even though it is not following it. For instance, if the present decision is regarded by the Court as a wise exception to a general line of precedents, it may seem better not to overrule.

Finally, the Court may "distinguish" between the instant case and the precedent. Since no two cases are exactly alike, this is relatively easy to do although not always convincing. The distinction between holding that baseball is not interstate commerce while boxing is,[28] is rather difficult for the naked (or layman's) eye to perceive; and "a repeatedly distinguished case," as Thomas Reed Powell has remarked, "is a case that is no longer distinguished"—so it loses its standing as precedent.

As in so many other instances, it becomes clear that the courts have a rather wide area of discretion in the use, nonuse, or misuse of precedent. To those who regard our courts as strictly legal agencies which, in Justice Roberts' words, merely "lay the article of the Constitution which is invoked beside the statute which is challenged and . . . decide whether the latter squares with the former," this rather cavalier approach to precedent is almost sacrilegious. But if courts are regarded as a part of the political process, it can hardly be argued that precedent should always be followed. One should perhaps draw a distinction here between those constitutional provisions that are clear and specific, such as the date of elections, and those that are general and ambiguous like the commerce clause. In cases involving the former, there is no room to ignore or change precedent as there is in those concerning the latter. A blind following of precedent would undoubtedly lead the Court into such difficulty that its powers of judicial review would be taken from it by the American people.

---

[26] See note 16, this chapter.

[27] *Hylton* v. *United States*, 3 Dallas 171 (1796).

[28] *Toolson* v. *New York Yankees*, 346 U.S. 356 (1953), and *United States* v. *International Boxing Club*, 348 U.S. 236 (1955).

The Supreme Court and the Lower Courts

When one considers that most Supreme Court cases come from lower courts and many of them return to lower courts, and, further, that the lower courts will have to handle many new cases by reference to previous decisions of the Supreme Court, it becomes clear that the relationships between the high court and other American courts are matters of some importance. This area can be but briefly treated here, in an attempt to point out some major considerations. Two major fields present themselves—the Supreme Court's attitude toward lower courts, and the attitudes and actions of the lower courts toward the Supreme Court.

The respect which the Supreme Court feels for certain courts or certain judges has apparently influenced it at times to accept their opinions without the close analysis it gives in cases coming from courts that do not command the same respect. This may be particularly true if the Court feels that the case is so difficult that it brought out the best in the lower court. In *Feiner* v. *New York*, Justice Frankfurter remarked, in a concurring opinion, that one of the reasons he was willing to uphold the decision of the New York court was that this particular court not only had considered the case carefully, but that it was a good court for which he had great respect. Since this court had a "good" record in civil liberties cases, Frankfurter obviously felt that more than ordinary deference was due its decision.

In considering the degree of respect to be given findings by the highest court of a State . . . the course of decisions by that court should be taken into account. . . . Only unfamiliarity with its decisions and the outlook of its judges could generate a notion that the Court of Appeals of New York is inhospitable to claims of civil liberties or is wanting in respect for this Court's decisions in support of them.[29]

Again, the *Dennis Communist Case* might be presented as an example. Chief Justice Fred M. Vinson was obviously impressed first of all by the fact that (he thought) Judge Harold Medina of the District Court had done a fine job under extremely difficult circumstances, which made him hesitant to be very critical. Second, he knew that the Circuit Court of the Second Circuit had the greatest prestige and the most respected jurists of any lower court in the United States (Judges Learned Hand, Augustus N. Hand, and Robert Patterson). And finally, he seemed somewhat awed by the fact that the opinion below had been written by Chief Judge Learned Hand, probably the most famous and respected of living American jurists, and a noted liberal as well.

Chief Justice Vinson wrote as though he were a little overwhelmed

---

[29] *Feiner* v. *New York*, 340 U.S. 315 (1951).

by the difficulty of the case and the reputation of Judge Hand. He quoted extensively both Medina's charge to the jury and Hand's opinion, and adopted Hand's destructive interpretation of the meaning of "clear and present danger" in the following respectful words:

> As articulated by Chief Judge Hand, it is as succinct and inclusive as any other we might devise at this time. It takes into consideration those factors which we deem relevant, and relates their significances. More we cannot expect from words.[30]

Several problems are posed by this approach. While it is impossible to suppose that justices would not be aware of the capabilities of their lower court colleagues, it is still somewhat doubtful that they should pay very much attention to this factor. How would the Court have decided the same case if it had *not* respected the lower courts? If John Doe had written the same opinion as Judge Learned Hand, would Chief Justice Vinson have accorded it the same respect? It does not seem a very good practice to pick and choose between lower court decisions on this basis, for it carries a clear implication that the very same lower court decision might be treated differently if the make-up of the court were different or if it came up from a different circuit. This appears to be a rather peculiar approach to constitutional law. It would seem more justifiable to judge the actions of lower courts not on their reputations but on the merit of the decision and opinion of each specific case. Even then the better lower court would score high in affirmances and low in reversals, but because it *was* a better court rather than because the Supreme Court *thought* it was.

As to the attitudes of the lower courts toward the Supreme Court, rather little study has been made, and comment must therefore be rather general. While all are aware of the general rule that lower courts must follow the decisions and precedents set by higher courts, it is sometimes not noted that even within this major limitation the trial and appellate courts, both state and federal, have large areas of discretion. This stems from two major factors. For one thing, as we have already seen, only a small minority of possible cases ever reach the Supreme Court; obviously, then, for questions that do not reach the high court the final answers are given somewhere lower in the judicial hierarchy, and the deciding courts have the same areas of discretion as the Supreme Court would have. In practice this is not as unfettered, for in addition to the normal limitations on court action which are outlined in Chapter IV, the lower courts are limited by the possible or actual rulings of the Supreme Court. Thus, if several circuit courts of appeals were to rule on the same question, which had not been previously decided by the Supreme Court, unless their decisions were all the same it is almost certain that the question

---

[30] *Dennis v. United States*, 341 U.S. 494 (1951).

would be taken up by the Supreme Court. The need of uniformity, as we have seen, is one of the reasons for granting certiorari.

But even after the Supreme Court has ruled on a question it is still possible for the lower courts to evade or avert the consequences of the higher court's ruling. The long record of evasion of court decision in the *Hawkins* cases is an illustration of this.[31] After all, the lower courts have the same ability to choose between precedents, to distinguish a case from its possible precedents, to use legal technicalities, and to "interpret" the precedents as does the Supreme Court itself. Subject to the overruling power of the Supreme Court, it is true that

. . . the subordinate judge's task of applying the Supreme Court's mandates is no more mechanical than is the Supreme Court's task of applying the Constitution's mandates. The high court decisions which are supposed to guide and control the subordinates are frequently just as ambiguous as is the Constitution or statute which is supposed to guide the Supreme Court, and they admit of many interpretations.[32]

The lower courts can use their powers, then, to limit or even to frustrate the decisions of the Supreme Court. As far as the parties to a case are concerned, winning in the Supreme Court may mean little, for the case may be returned to a lower court for further action, as the phrase goes, "not inconsistent with this opinion." And since the Supreme Court may well have decided a point of law rather than the case itself, the lower court on rehearing may find that the Supreme Court's ruling on the legal point does not have the effect of changing the original decision in the case.

It is clear that the Supreme Court's relationships with the lower courts are neither simple nor one-way. What the law is in practice depends not only on what the Supreme Court says it is, but also to some extent on what the lower courts say the Supreme Court said.

Suggestions for Further Reading

The Jurisdiction of the Supreme Court

Most of the literature on jurisdiction is excessively technical for the purposes of the political scientist. Perhaps best from this standpoint, because written by a political scientist, is Robert J. Harris, *The Judicial Power of the United States* (Baton Rouge: Louisiana State University Press, 1940). See also Charles W. Bunn, *Jurisdiction*

---

[31] See note 19, this chapter.
[32] Jack W. Peltason, *Federal Courts in the Political Process* (Garden City: Doubleday & Co., 1955), p. 14.

and Practice of the Courts of the United States (5th ed.; St. Paul, Minn.: West Publishing Co., 1949); Felix Frankfurter and James M. Landis, *The Business of the Supreme Court* (New York: The Macmillan Co., 1927); Reynolds Robertson and Francis R. Kirkham, *Jurisdiction of the Supreme Court* (Albany, N.Y.: Matthew Bender & Co., 1951); Charles Evans Hughes, *The Supreme Court of the United States* (New York: Columbia University Press, 1928). An excellent general treatment of the legal system of the United States may be found in Lewis Mayers, *The American Legal System* (New York: Harper & Brothers, 1955).

Certain special aspects of Supreme Court practice are helpfully discussed in Oliver P. Field, *The Effect of an Unconstitutional Statute* (Minneapolis: University of Minnesota Press, 1935); Charles G. Post, *The Supreme Court and Political Questions* (Baltimore: Johns Hopkins Press, 1936); Mitchell Wendell, *Relations between the Federal and State Courts* (New York: Columbia University Press, 1949).

The rules of the Supreme Court on appeals and certiorari are Rules 15 and 23; they are reprinted in Vol. 74 of the *Supreme Court Reporter* (1953).

The Case in Court

Perhaps the best contemporary picture of the Supreme Court at work is given in Alpheus T. Mason's definitive biography, *Harlan Fiske Stone, Pillar of the Law* (New York: The Viking Press, 1956); see also John P. Frank, *Marble Palace* (New York: Alfred A. Knopf, 1958). There is a great deal of scattered periodical literature as well; particularly helpful might be the annual summary of the Court's work (with accompanying articles) which are published in the *Harvard Law Review* each November; somewhat similar comments appear annually in *The American Political Science Review*. Most of the works mentioned in the above paragraphs are relevant here as well.

In General

There is extensive periodical literature covering various of the points discussed in this chapter. Much of it, unfortunately, is highly technical, as well as being inaccessible except in law school libraries. Nevertheless it may be of help to the student to list a few relevant and useful articles.

Beth, Loren P. "Technical and Doctrinal Aids to Constitutional Interpretation," 18 *Univ. of Pittsburgh Law Rev.* 108 (1956).

Blaustein, Albert P., and Field, Andrew H. " 'Overruling' Opinions in the Supreme Court," 57 *Michigan Law Rev.* 151 (1958).

Borchard, Edwin. "The Federal Declaratory Judgment Act," 21 *Virginia Law Rev.* 35 (1934).

Boudin, Louis B. "The Problem of Stare Decisis in Our Constitutional Theory," 8 *New York Univ. Law Qtrly.* 589 (1931).

Corwin, Edward S. "Judicial Review in Action," 74 *Univ. of Pennsylvania Law Rev.* 639 (1926).

Culp, Maurice S. "Methods of Attacking Unconstitutional Legislation," 22 *Virginia Law Rev.* 723, 891 (1936).

Diamond, Sidney A. "Federal Jurisdiction to Decide Moot Cases," 94 *Univ. of Pennsylvania Law Rev.* 125 (1946).

Dodd, Walter F. "Implied Powers and Implied Limitations," 29 *Yale Law Jnl.* 137 (1919).

————. "Judicially Nonenforceable Provisions of Constitutions," 80 *Univ. of Pennsylvania Law Rev.* 54 (1931).

Gibbs, Robert W. "Certiorari: Its Diagnosis and Cure," 6 *Hastings Law Jnl.* 131 (1955).

Grant, J. A. C. "The Natural Law Background of Due Process," 31 *Columbia Law Rev.* 56 (1931).

Hanna, John. "The Role of Precedent in Judicial Decision," 2 *Villanova Law Rev.* 367 (1957).

Harlan, John M. "What Part Does the Oral Argument Play in the Conduct of an Appeal?" 41 *Cornell Law Qtrly.* 6 (1955).

Leflar, Robert A. "The Task of the Appellate Court," 33 *Notre Dame Lawyer* 548 (1958).

Leiman, Joan. "The Rule of Four," 57 *Columbia Law Rev.* 975 (1957).

Levitan, Mortimer. "Dissertation on Writing Legal Opinions," 1960 *Wisconsin Law Rev.* 22.

London, Ernest J. " 'Federal Question' Jurisdiction—A Snare and a Delusion," 57 *Michigan Law Rev.* 835 (1959).

Morse, Oliver. "Judicial Self-Denial and Judicial Activism: The Personality of the Original Jurisdiction of the District Courts," 3 *Cleveland-Marshall Law Rev.* 101 (1954); 4, 7 (1955).

Pound, Roscoe. "Spurious Interpretation," 7 *Columbia Law Rev.* 397 (1907).

Rheinstein, Max. "The Constitutional Bases of Jurisdiction," 22 *Univ. of Chicago Law Rev.* 775 (1955).

Steamer, Robert J. "The Role of the Federal District Courts in the Segregation Controversy," 22 *Jnl. of Politics* 417 (1960).

Tate, Phyllis M., and Holzer, Henri M. "The Supreme Court and Standing to Sue," 34 *New York Univ. Law Qtrly.* 141 (1959).

ten Broek, Jacobus. "Use by the Supreme Court of Extrinsic Aids in Constitutional Construction," 26 *California Law Rev.* 287, 437, 664 (1938); and 27, 157, 399 (1939).

Wickersham, Cornelius W. "The Supreme Court and Federal Criminal Procedure," 44 *Cornell Law Qtrly.* 14 (1958).

ZoBell, Karl M. "Division of Opinion in the Supreme Court: A History of Judicial Disintegration," 44 *Cornell Law Qtrly.* 186 (1959).

Comment: "Disposition of Moot Cases by the United States Supreme Court," 23 *Univ. of Chicago Law Rev.* 77 (1955).

Comment: "Supreme Court No-Clear-Majority Decisions: A Study in Stare Decisis," 24 *Univ. of Chicago Law Rev.* 99 (1956).

Comment: "The Three-Judge Federal Court in Constitutional Litigation: A Procedural Anachronism," 27 *Univ. of Chicago Law Rev.* 555 (1960).

Note: "Supreme Court Per Curiam Practices: A Critique," 69 *Harvard Law Rev.* 707 (1956).

Note: "Per Curiam Decisions of the Supreme Court: 1957 Term," 26 *Univ. of Chicago Law Rev.* 279 (1959).

CHAPTER IV

The Courts as
Political Agents:
A General Analysis

Scarcely any political question arises in the United States that is not resolved, sooner or later, into a judicial question.

—ALEXIS DE TOCQUEVILLE, *Democracy in America*

While there have always been perceptive observers who disagreed, the common idea about the Supreme Court before the 1930's was that it was a strictly legal body, deliberately and completely divorced from politics, and permanently stationed on some judicial Mt. Sinai, from which constitutional judgments issued forth on tablets of stone like the Ten Commandments. Lord Bryce, the famous British political scientist, wrote in 1888 that American judges:

. . . simply interpret the law. The word "control" is misleading, because it implies that the person or body of whom it is used possesses and exerts discretionary personal Will. Now the American judges have no will in the matter. . . . The will that prevails is the will of the people, expressed in the Constitution which they had enacted—all that the judges have to do is to discover from the enactments before them what the will of the people is, and apply that will to the facts of a given case.[1]

And James M. Beck, U.S. Attorney General under Coolidge, wrote in much the same vein:

---

[1] James Bryce, *The American Commonwealth* (3rd ed.; New York: The Macmillan Co., 1893), Vol. I, p. 252.

In the judicial department of the government, the judge is rarely influenced by pragmatic considerations. He believes that he is charged with the solemn duty of administering great principles of law, which often involve questions of eternal justice. He is not concerned with what the majority think of the principle nor necessarily of the immediate practical effects of its application.[2]

More sophisticated commentators, particularly in recent years, have often gone to the other extreme, indicating a belief that the judges of the Court are active politicians with one eye on the voters when they decide particular cases, or that they decide entirely on the basis of personal predilections on social or economic matters. Brooks Adams has well expressed these ideas.

. . . [F]rom the outset, the American bench, because it deals with the most fiercely contested of political issues, has been an instrument necessary to political success. Consequently, political parties have striven to control it, and therefore the bench has always had an avowed partisan bias.

. . . [T]he American constitutional system . . . breeds in the judge the conviction that he is superior to the legislator. His instinct, under adequate pressure, is always to overrule anything repugnant to him that a legitimate legislative assembly may have done.[3]

While neither version, of course, is wholly true, the actuality seems to lie somewhat nearer the sophisticated approach than the naïve one. A more accurate statement of the function of the Supreme Court would deny that its members are politicians in the usual sense of that much-abused word, or that it ordinarily allows the personal convictions of its members to govern its decisions completely; but it would admit that the Court is in the highest sense political—that it plays a vital role in the processes by which the policies pursued by American governments are decided.

Judicial Review as Politics

It would perhaps be extreme to say that no law or other governmental policy is complete until it receives judicial approval, for many actions are so obviously constitutional, or so noncontroversial, that they are not challenged in the courts. For any governmental act, however, there may be said to be at least a *potential* court review, and practically all important and controversial policy decisions sooner or later come before the courts. Consequently the judicial veto is just as much a part of the policy-making process as is the presidential veto. To be

---

[2] James M. Beck, *The Changed Conception of the Constitution* (Rochester: University of Rochester, 1925), p. 55.

[3] Brooks Adams, *The Theory of Social Revolutions* (New York: The Macmillan Co., 1913), pp. 47, 125.

sure, it is essentially a negative power: in the exercise of judicial review the courts do not ordinarily affirmatively *make* policy. Rather, they *allow policy to be made* (if the act is upheld) or negate policy (if it is voided). It is still up to the "political" branches of the government to decide, in most instances, what policies shall be pursued, within whatever limitations the courts might impose.

But even such a negative power has positive implications, just as the executive veto does. These implications lie partly in the threat of the veto. Congress must always (and so must all other governmental officials) keep one eye on the Supreme Court in making policy. It must try to make sure that the policies enacted will be able successfully to run the judicial gauntlet. To do this, the policy makers in Congress must be familiar with past Court decisions and with present trends in the courts. In this indirect fashion it may be said that the courts do play a positive role in the fashioning of policy. Thus the Supreme Court's overturning of the first Agricultural Adjustment Act in 1936[4] was directly instrumental in fashioning the revised version of the same law which was passed by Congress as the second AAA in 1938. President Truman's actions in trying to solve the steel strike of 1952 were similarly conditioned by the Court's ruling in the *Steel Seizure Case* of that year,[5] as will be the actions of future presidents on problems of similar nature. Also, even a negative decision, such as the one outlawing racial segregation, may have extremely significant positive policy implications: for desegregation is not a no-man's land; it requires integration.

The significance of judicial review cannot be judged solely in terms of the frequency of its use, or of the importance of the cases in which it is exercised. Any estimate of its role in the American political process must take account also of the intangible element involved in the *threat* of its use: it acts as an omnipresent censor, restricting the things that are actually done and the way in which they are done even when they are not formally adjudicated. Laws passed by Congress express the judgment of the legislators as to what is politically and abstractly wise, or even as to what is constitutional; they also express an educated legislative guess as to the probable attitude of the courts.

Keeping all this in mind, however, it nevertheless seems likely that the principal policy-making function of the courts—at least in the realm of *national* government action—lies in statutory interpretation, not in judicial review. It is hard to list many specific instances in which Congress or the national executive has found it necessary to refrain from taking an important policy step because of legal fears; such fears may affect the form of governmental action, but they do not often affect its substance.

---

[4] *United States* v. *Butler*, 297 U.S. 1 (1936).
[5] *Youngstown Sheet & Tube Co.* v. *Sawyer*, 343 U.S. 579 (1952).

Statutory Interpretation by Courts

Much of the influence of the judiciary on the making of national policy, then, comes through the power of statutory interpretation rather than through judicial review. Every law passed must be applied, and its application is to a large extent dependent on what administrators and judges think it means.

Especially in modern times, few laws are passed which are so simple that their entire meaning is self-evident and needs no interpretation. A hypothetical example will illustrate this point. Suppose that the city council passes an ordinance forbidding driving over twenty-five miles per hour in "any residential area within the city limits." On first appraisal this appears to be a very simple law with no complications and not open to misunderstanding. But a little thought will present questions. Driving what? Any kind of wheeled vehicle, or only automobiles? What is a "residential area"? Must all the occupied property be residential or can it be mixed? Is an unoccupied area residential? Or do you merely follow the zoning ordinances (if any) on this matter?

These questions will almost surely be presented to the courts sooner or later. The court may say that a particular defendant is not guilty, since he was driving in a zone that contained no buildings and therefore was not in a "residential area." If there is no particular objection to this interpretation, it becomes for all practical purposes a part of the ordinance. If, on the other hand, the city council disapproves of the court's interpretation, it may clarify the ordinance by amendment. In either case, the court has played an important part in determining the practical meaning of the law.

The more complex a law is—and complex laws are the typical ones today—the more significant the role of the courts becomes. Complex laws, or those dealing with complex situations, consequently, are partly or even largely made by the courts in the process of attempting to apply them.

Such a complex law—dealing with the interrelationships of our entire economic system—is the Fair Labor Standards Act of 1938.[6] This law may serve as an illustration of the process of statutory interpretation. The law provides for minimum wages, maximum hours, overtime pay, and other matters for employees "engaged in the production of goods for [interstate] commerce." The law originally defined this as including all employees engaged in "any process or occupation necessary to the production of goods for commerce." [7] The courts were soon asked to decide such questions as whether window washers cleaning windows in Detroit auto plants were covered by the

---

[6] 52 *Stat.* 1060 (1938), 29 U.S.C.A. §201 *et seq.* (1938).
[7] *Ibid.*, §203 (*j*) (1938).

act;[8] whether elevator operators in the national offices of the Borden Company were covered;[9] and (since people "employed in agriculture" were exempted) whether office employees of a farmers' co-operative irrigation project were covered.[10]

After some years of litigation on this act, complaints began to reach Congress from various commercial interests that the law was being applied by administrators and courts to businesses beyond its proper scope. Congress therefore undertook to clarify the law; instead of "necessary to" production, the law was changed to read "in any closely related process or occupation directly essential" to production.[11] So the courts had to start out anew, trying to interpret the meaning of a clause written to clarify a previous clause!

Such cases not only are not unusual, they are typical. How a law is applied is as important as what it says. And thus, in the field of federal governmental action, court interpretation of statutes, executive orders, or administrative rulings may play a large role in the way these actually affect the citizen. As Chief Justice Hughes once wrote, "a federal statute finally means what the Court says it means."

Judicial Control of Administrative Agencies

It has been suggested above that judicial review includes not only review of legislation, but of other acts of government as well. One of the most significant fields of judicial activity in recent years, because of the great growth of government regulation of varied human enterprises, has been connected with the agencies set up to administer these regulations. The system of administrative regulation and services is so vast that it is difficult to form a clear impression of it. It includes not only the so-called "regulatory" agencies themselves, such as the Interstate Commerce Commission and the National Labor Relations Board, but also some of the activities of practically every government bureau. The admission practices of immigration officials; the granting of old-age pensions by the Social Security Board, or of passports by the State Department; "GI Bill" benefits handled by the Veterans Administration; and countless other government activities that affect the rights and privileges of Americans—all are involved.

Administrative agencies work within at least a double framework, the outlines of which are supplied by the Constitution and by the laws governing their operations. Consequently both judicial review and

---

[8] *Martino v. Michigan Window Cleaning Co.*, 327 U.S. 173 (1946).

[9] *Borden Co. v. Borella*, 325 U.S. 679 (1945).

[10] *Farmers' Reservoir and Irrigation Co. v. MacComb*, 337 U.S. 755 (1949).

[11] 52 *Stat.* 1060 (1938), 29 U.S.C.A. §203 (j) (1938), as amended (1949).

statutory interpretation are important. Constitutionally, probably the most significant aspect is the use of the due process clauses as a means of checking the procedures used by governmental agencies. For instance, in *Reilly* v. *Pinkus* the Supreme Court invalidated an order refusing post-office privileges to the makers of "Kelp-I-Dine" on the grounds that it was not a valuable reducing agent in the sense in which it was advertised. The evidence against the company had been presented in the hearing by two medical specialists who used medical text statements to back up their opinions, but the company had been refused the opportunity to cross-examine them or to present other texts which said the opposite. The Supreme Court held that the lack of the right to cross-examine constituted an absence of due process, and set aside the order.[12]

Here, as in the more general instances introduced above, statutory interpretation is more commonly used than judicial review. Every government agency operates under a mass of general and specific laws which govern its field of operation, its powers within that field, its modes of procedure, and its organization. These laws require interpretation just as do any other laws, and the interpretations used affect deeply the daily lives of millions of citizens. Thousands of instances of this could be cited. In 1908 the Supreme Court decided a case involving the question whether the Interstate Commerce Commission could force witnesses to appear and testify before it as part of a general investigation to see whether laws were being violated. The law under which the ICC operated said that it could require testimony "for the purposes of this act." Justice Holmes, speaking for the Court, said that this phrase did not include the forcing of testimony except in connection with specific charges of violations of the Interstate Commerce Act. Thus the subpoena power of the ICC was narrowly restricted, and "fishing expeditions" by the agency rendered impossible.[13] This one illustration would be enough to indicate that the courts as well as Congress have a great deal to do with the extent and meaning *in practice* of government administered programs of regulation or service.

Judicial Review of State Governmental Action

Possibly the major significance of judicial review is to be found not in the review of federal governmental action, but in review of the acts of state and municipal governments. This fact seems to result from two considerations. First, the very multiplicity of governments involved—fifty states and innumerable sub-state governmental units—leads logi-

---

[12] *Reilly* v. *Pinkus*, 338 U.S. 269 (1949).

[13] Justice Oliver Wendell Holmes in *Harriman* v. *Interstate Commerce Commission*, 211 U.S. 407 (1908).

cally to the much greater possibility of constitutional infractions. Second, conditions bound up in the American political framework make our smaller governments more prone to excess than our larger ones. Checks and balances supplied by the multiplicity of groups and interests will work better the more such groups and interests there are; consequently small jurisdictions are more likely to fall under the domination of single factions which, because of lack of effective opposition, may be politically powerful enough to violate constitutional provisions. It should be remembered in this connection that a great deal of constitutional litigation centers around the use of the "police powers" of the states, and most police power legislation is state or local. Justice Holmes was probably thinking of these facts when he penned his striking phrase: "I do not think the United States would come to an end if we lost our power to declare an act of Congress void. I do think the Union would be imperilled if we could not make that declaration as to the laws of the several states."

The review of state governmental action is not limited to review of laws passed by state legislatures. It includes much more: review of the provisions of state constitutions; review of acts of state executive officials or administrative agencies; review of state court decisions; review of acts of county, city, school board, police officials, prosecuting attorneys, etc. In other words, any action by a state, a state official, or a state agency that is alleged to violate any provision of the federal Constitution may be reviewed by the Supreme Court. Such review has probably always been more important both in quantity and in significance than the similar review granted as to federal actions, as this text will amply illustrate.

The one reservation perhaps needed to this comment is that with the rise of modern positive government at the national level it has become more likely that the federal government will transgress constitutional limitations. As the balance of federal-state power shifts, in other words, so may the balance of the importance of the two aspects of judicial review.

Judicial Review of Actions by Lower Courts

An aspect of judicial review of particular significance in the area of trial rights and court procedures comes as a result of the normal appellate processes, which culminate, for some federal cases and for state cases that involve federal constitutional questions, in the United States Supreme Court. Thus, if a lower court refuses a defendant the right to cross-examine witnesses, or violates any other provision contained in the Bill of Rights or implied by due process of law, the aggrieved party may apply to the Supreme Court for redress. The significance of this aspect of judicial review is difficult to overemphasize.

At bottom our civil liberties are based both historically and logically on the right to a fair trial under regular processes of the law and for violation of known laws. Such rights as habeas corpus, cross-examination, the right to counsel and to the observance of the rules of evidence are often regarded as the basic rights of a free community, for they prevent governments from abusing legal procedures in order to remove their opponents from circulation. The preservation of fair procedures in all of our courts is a responsibility both of our legislatures and of the courts themselves, and review in this field by the highest court is thus of extreme importance. This is the major bulwark we have against the use of police-state methods such as those used in totalitarian nations.

In this connection it should also be noted that to function properly in protecting citizens against arbitrary trial and imprisonment, the independence of judges from the "political" authorities is a prime requisite. Where, as in sixteenth-century England, the courts are the King's courts, no justice is possible unless the King wills it. The same was true of the "people's courts" of the French Revolution, and those of Hitler and of the Communists. The foundation for fair trial lies in such constitutional provisions as life tenure for judges—which supplies another reason why state actions are more likely to violate the Constitution than are federal actions, since most state judges do not have life tenure, but are elected and thus "democratically" responsive to public pressures.

Pressure Groups and the Courts

Those who are familiar with the operation of the American political system will need no reminder that pressure groups exist to influence governmental policy in the directions favored by the particular group. If the thesis of this chapter is correct—that the American court system is an important part of the policy-making process—it follows that pressure groups will attempt to influence court action, just as they attempt to sway policy decisions in the legislative and executive branches.

Since the courts are bound to the case system, since judges are not elected but hold office for life, and since court action must always be set in a legal framework, interest groups cannot approach the courts by the use of the same methods that would be appropriate in approaching Congress. There are no campaign funds and no ballot boxes with which to influence judges. And the federal court system is so highly professionalized, with a code of ethics so strong, that bribery and coercion are rendered highly improbable if not impossible. In the appellate courts the ordinary approaches are made even more difficult by the practice of using collegial panels instead of single judges, which has the effect of reinforcing the strength of the ethical code.

There remain only two practical methods by which pressure may be exerted on the courts. The first of these is through the appointment of judges. Influence in this field, however, must proceed indirectly through the President and the Senate. It is therefore extremely difficult to detect whatever pressure-group influence may exist. It seems probable that any conscious or deliberate pressure is ineffective; but the unconscious pressures flowing through the normal processes of politics are no doubt of great importance. Some of these will be discussed a little farther on.

The other means by which to approach the courts is through the regular procedure of litigation. This is clearly more important than the selection of judges. Even though the federal courts have repeatedly refused to issue advisory opinions, it is seldom very difficult to get to court with a case. In consequence, the question of the constitutionality or proper interpretation of any law to which a pressure group (or even an individual) is opposed is almost sure to reach the courts sooner or later.

Several things should be noted about this mode of pressure-group activity. In the first place, it is largely defensive in nature, especially where constitutional questions are involved. This means that in most cases, by the time the group is forced to resort to the courts, a policy has already been made by the legislative and executive branches—and thus the hope of the interest group is that the policy may be negated by the court's decision. Thus, when the coal mining companies failed to prevent the passage of the Guffey Coal Act during the New Deal era, they turned to the courts and were successful in persuading the judges that the act was an unconstitutional regulation of commerce which came properly under state jurisdiction.

If an election is lost [said Brooks Adams], and the legislature, which has been chosen by the majority, cannot be pacified by money, . . . the first instinct of the capitalist is to retain counsel, not to advise him touching his duty under the law, but to devise a method by which he may elude it, or, if he cannot elude it, by which he may have it annulled as unconstitutional by the courts.[14]

It goes without saying that "the first instinct of the capitalist" is also the first instinct of any other group disadvantaged by legislative enactments.

There are, however, cases in which pressure-group activity in the courts is not of a defensive nature only. It may often happen that the interpretation of a statute is more important to the group than its mere presence on the statute books. The group may in such a case try

---

[14] Adams, *op. cit.*, pp. 213–14.

to force its desires on the administrative officials enforcing the law by getting the courts to declare that the desired interpretation is actually the proper one.

Again, in constitutional cases it may be that a particular group aggressively tries to foster a new constitutional concept in order to advance its own interests which, for some reason, it has failed to secure through the more normal political channels. Thus the National Association for the Advancement of Colored People for many years—and with much success—has actively sought in the courts a broadened interpretation of the Fourteenth Amendment so as to achieve goals which, under American political conditions, it could not obtain either from the Congress or from many of the state governments.

Another aspect of pressure-group activity in the courts is its adversary nature. Much of the time there are one or more pressure groups directly or indirectly involved on each side of a policy question. In the *Guffey Coal Act Case*, the coal companies opposed the act while the miners' unions favored it. However, it is not often that both sides can get directly before the courts, and in the case mentioned the companies took both sides just to get the case to court! More normally the government is one of the parties to the case, thus tacitly representing one set of interests. In many cases outside groups not parties to the case may be allowed to present arguments in the role of *amici curiae* —"friends of the court."

In one extremely important sense the interplay between courts and interest groups is a distinct and valuable addition to the democratic political process. This stems from the fact that it is almost as easy for a single individual or very small group to go before the courts as it is for a large and powerful interest to do so. The influencing of legislative and executive policy, on the other hand, is largely dependent on the size, strength, or wealth of the group. Thus the small and weak— groups that are by definition almost powerless in a democracy—can often obtain a hearing and some sort of justice from the courts which they could not get from the "political" branches of government. No better illustrations are needed than two sets of recent cases in which weak and persecuted groups have found the courts of great value: the Jehovah's Witnesses cases and the antidiscrimination cases presented by the NAACP.

For the same reasons, the courts may on occasion be handy instruments for the protection of once-powerful groups whose political power has declined. Thomas Jefferson, as early as 1801, charged the Federalists with "retiring into the battlement of the judiciary" to defeat his policies. And, defeated in the legislature, corporate interests have often turned to the courts, as in the *Income Tax Case* of 1895, in which Joseph H. Choate urged at the bar of the Supreme Court that it was the Court's duty to "stand in the breach" against the advancing tide of Communism, even if Congress and the President would not.[15] There is some evidence that substantive due process as a protection of corporations lives on in many of our state courts long after the federal courts have rejected it.

It should be noted at this point that the "stockholder's suit," by which a stockholder may sue his company in order to force it to disobey the law (as in the *Guffey Coal Act Case* mentioned above), has provided corporations with a relatively easy way of getting to court; but means of litigation are so varied in any case that obtaining a court hearing is not really a major problem if reasonable care is exercised in preparing the proper case. It is carelessness, for instance, that accounts for the Supreme Court's refusal to hear a public school Bible-reading case because it was based on the grievance of a parent whose child had graduated from school before the case wound its tortuous way up to the Court, thus rendering the issue "moot." [16] Careful lawyers would have seen to it that the parent selected as a legal vehicle had children young enough so that it was unlikely they would graduate before the case found its way through the courts.

A final almost intangible factor should be mentioned. Most pressure-group influence in the courts is not really "influence" in the usual sense of the word. The "influence," in practice, is the influence of logic and reason—a carefully prepared and well-argued case—rather than that of obvious propaganda or ballot box threat. Not only this, but to a large extent the law has always been a conservative force in society. Therefore the courts tend to be conservative—a factor that is reinforced by the advanced ages of judges and the fact that most lawyers are largely business-oriented. In long periods of our history conservative interest groups have been able to get what they wanted from the courts *without exerting any influence* beyond the mere presentation of a case. That is, the courts held the same beliefs, valuations, and predispositions as the conservative groups. All that was needed, then, was to litigate. This may, of course, sometimes be true of nonconservative groups as well. What this means is that courts may not need to be convinced, for they may already have the conviction; but the nature of the legal process means that they must wait for someone to bring them the question in the proper legal form.

This comment is subject to a stringent qualification, however, since as we have already seen, in the long run courts must abide by the verdict of public opinion if they cannot shape it, or run the risk of having their power diluted.

---

[15] *Pollock* v. *Farmers' Loan and Trust Co.*, 158 U.S. 601 (1895).
[16] *Doremus* v. *Board of Education*, 342 U.S. 429 (1952).

The Importance of Discretion on the Supreme Court

All that has been said in the foregoing pages has been based on the assumption that a judge is not just an automatic legal reflex mechanism, but that he holds a great deal of discretionary power in his hands. And while this discretion is not unlimited (as will be emphasized below), it is yet sufficiently broad to be of great significance both in constitutional and in statutory interpretation. Only such discretion would give the courts a significant policy-making role, or any power sufficient to attract the interest of pressure groups in their decisions.

If constitutional and statutory provisions were of self-evident meaning, courts would be of no significance in the policy field. But such self-evidence is seldom possible and often not even desirable. Modern regulatory statutes by design leave many details to be filled in by interpretation. And the American Constitution has often been praised for the wise generality of many of its provisions. This generality leaves a great deal of latitude for the discretion of judges; and it is the provisions of general nature that are subjected to most constitutional litigation.

The most difficult problem involved in the use of such discretion by a "nonpolitical" and "irresponsible" agency is the likelihood that it will degenerate into merely the personal opinions of the judges written into law. Judges have often been accused—by lawyers, laymen, politicians, and their own colleagues—of doing just that. In fact it is difficult to see how such judicial lawmaking can be completely avoided. Judges, after all, are not slot machines automatically giving certain answers to certain questions. They are, on the contrary, only too human, subject to the foibles, inconsistencies, prejudices, and preconceptions common to all men. They grow up in ordinary families, attend the public schools, are trained in the law schools, and many spend full careers of political endeavor before reaching the bench. How could one expect them suddenly to ascend Mt. Olympus, divorcing themselves from all that they had previously believed and striven to achieve? Do judges make law? An old Vermont judge wisely replied, " 'Course they do—made some myself."

Justice Robert H. Jackson, an unusually acute (if somewhat inconsistent) member of the Supreme Court from 1942 to 1954, has cogently discussed this general question in the following words:

. . . [A]s an advocate at the Supreme Court bar in many constitutional cases, I never was able to determine what material would really be considered by the several Justices as controlling of such issues. And I am bound to admit that a decade of experience as a judge throws little more light on the problem. Nothing has more perplexed generations of conscientious judges than the search in juridical science, philosophy and practice for objective and impersonal criteria for solution of politico-legal questions put to our courts. Few judges like to be accused of acting from merely personal predilections. Yet, frequently that is the point of dissenting opinions. Confusion at the bar and disagreement on the bench usually begin in lack of an accepted system of weights and measures to mete out constitutional justice. Unfortunately, the conclusion of judges having the highest sense of professional responsibility is that the present state of our constitutional development provides no definitive principles of decision.

We start, of course, with the constitutional text. But if that makes the answer clear, there is no problem. It is the imprecise, obscure or ambiguous state of the text that raises the issue. So where do we go next?

[To precedents? They are] accepted only at their current valuation and have a mortality rate almost as high as their authors.

[To natural law or "realism"? Both] shield the judge with an impersonal and probably unconscious camouflage for holdings that emerge out of the mists of preconception.

Exclude as far as possible the pressure of group opinion, but let us not deceive ourselves; long-sustained public opinion does influence the process of constitutional interpretation. Each new member of the ever-changing personnel of our courts brings to his task the assumptions and accustomed thought of a later period. The practical play of the forces of politics is such that judicial power has often delayed but never permanently defeated the persistent will of a substantial majority. Judicial review in practice therefore has proved less an obstacle to majority rule than the followers of Mr. Jefferson feared and less a guaranty of the *status quo* than the followers of Mr. Hamilton hoped.

Justice Jackson concluded with a statement of his beliefs as to the proper attitudes of a judge working under such difficulties.

. . . [O]ur conclusions, fallible though they are and mistaken though they may be, [should] represent a real respect and aspiration for law, a faithful effort to apply law and a veneration for the work of the great minds that have made our legal structure the nearest to a safeguard of freedom that has been devised.[17]

A conscientious judge is faced with the problem of subordinating his own beliefs and valuations as far as is humanly possible, even though his job involves answering questions the nature of which makes *complete* neutrality an impossibility. As will appear, some judges have been more successful than others in this endeavor, and some have not even been conscious of the problem. But no judge—not even he who has wrestled most manfully—has completely succeeded in divorcing his desires from his decisions.

It would be easy to proceed from this statement to the conclusion that judicial review is an oligarchic and harmful encumbrance to democracy; and that if we are to be governed by will and opinion anyway, it had best be that of a representative legislature rather than that of an unrepresentative court. This, though, would ignore the arguments of Chapter II as well as the severe limitations on judicial discretion which we have yet to discuss. Judges do not live in a political

[17] Robert H. Jackson (speech to the American Bar Association, Boston, August 24, 1953), *Vital Speeches*, XIX, No. 24 (October 1, 1953), 759.

vacuum which leaves them wholly free to decide as they please; on the contrary, there are many forces that help—or even compel—them in certain directions. To these forces we will turn in a moment.

The Distinction between Judicial and Legislative Policy Making

Although the fact that the judiciary plays an important part in the policy-making process has been emphasized in this chapter—a part so significant that it is sometimes spoken of as "judicial legislation"—it does not follow that judicial policy making is the same, either in form or in content, as legislation.

The most obvious distinction is that legislation is ordinarily *general* in nature and *prospective* in effect; that is, it is the formulation of a general rule which will apply in the future to many specific cases. Court decisions, on the other hand, are usually *specific* and *retrospective* in that they settle disputes that have already taken place. Consequently, the policy emerging from the judicial process is not labeled as "legislation," and its content must be at least partially gleaned from speculation as to future decisions in similar but not identical cases. Of course discerning judges have realized for centuries that their decisions have an effect far beyond the ruling in the specific case; in instances such as the *School Segregation Cases* this is too manifest to require comment. But this effect comes from the assumption that like cases in the future will be decided the same way. In other words, the decision is given, by lawyers and the public, a more general and prospective effect than it formally contains. Even so it cannot be equated with legislation in this respect.

Another distinction, referred to earlier, is the generally negative character of court decision. On the whole, courts do not initiate or invent policies, but pass upon policies coming from somewhere else. Then too, courts are passive rather than active instruments of policy. That is, they do not actively reach out, investigate, and write laws or decide to void them. On the contrary, they must allow the law to be written elsewhere; and after it is written they must depend on the forces of political opposition to bring a case to them for adjudication. A law may be ever so unconstitutional; it will nevertheless remain on the books unless someone brings it before the courts for a ruling. Most commentators, for instance, believe that the Sedition Act of 1798 was unconstitutional, but no court ever said so, because no one ever tested it in court.

Courts, as has already been pointed out, are not subject to the same modes of pressure-group activity as are the legislatures. Nor do party politics mean the same thing or work the same way where courts are concerned. This is not to say that "party" makes no difference in the courts, but that the forces of partisanship, like interest groups, must operate in different ways.

Finally, it should be well understood by now that the framework of legislative action—organization, party, pressure group, public opinion, elections—is radically different or nonexistent in the milieu of the courts. Thus even though one may properly speak of "judicial policy making," it must be kept in mind that it is not only policy making but also judicial: that it cannot be studied as if it were the same thing as policy making by some other agency. The courts do play an indispensable part in the making of policy, but it is not the same part that is played by the legislature or the executive.

Lawyers and the Courts

The ideas and arguments of lawyers contribute much in determining the direction of legal interpretation. The significance of these contributions can be underscored by recalling the large amount of discretion involved in judicial decision making. If courts had no element of choice, legal argument would be of slight importance. Then too, the great weight of the legal profession in the whole of American life makes the ideas of lawyers peculiarly liable to reflect the feelings of dominant segments of society.

As early as the 1830's commentators recognized the lawyer's importance in civic and ideological leadership in this country. Lawyers then were as a class the best educated men in every community. They also had in their favor the existence of the common law, which makes litigation and the aid of lawyers more essential than in most other legal systems. In addition, lawyers in a democracy have a natural affinity for politics and thus readily become political leaders.

In later times the significance of the legal profession has been due not to its education—which may not be as good in some respects as that of other professions or groups—but rather to the continued preeminence of lawyers in democratic politics and to the strategic position lawyers occupy in mediating between the lay public and the extraordinary and growing complexities of modern positive law.

Whatever the reasons, there is no doubt that the members of the federal bar have played large roles in the shaping of constitutional doctrines from Marshall's day to the present. One need only recall a few examples to prove the point. It has been said that Chief Justice John Marshall in some of his greatest opinions largely paraphrased the arguments of counsel at bar, such as those of Daniel Webster in *Gibbons* v. *Ogden*.[18] The parts played by John A. Campbell, Roscoe

---

[18] *Gibbons* v. *Ogden*, 9 Wheaton 1 (1824).

Conkling, and Joseph H. Choate in the development of the substantive concept of due process of law and liberty of contract have been analyzed by several historians. And the successful development by lawyer Louis D. Brandeis of the fact-laden "Brandeis brief" (which presented social and economic data rather than only legal arguments) is a famous example.

It should be remembered when considering this point, however, that the judges always have alternative choices: there are always two sides to a case, and two sets of lawyers' briefs. The lawyer who is most successful is likely to be the one who is best able to play to the already existing attitudes of the judges, or slowly—as did Campbell— to help build up in them a new set of attitudes.

Before leaving the subject, a rather significant development of the last fifty years should be noted. Although legal commentators such as Justice Joseph Story, Chancellor James Kent, and Judge Thomas M. Cooley were of tremendous importance in influencing the course of constitutional development during the nineteenth century, in general the more significant factor was the argument at the bar. Since about 1900, however, with the development and institutionalization of formal legal training, the law school teacher and the law review have played increasingly significant roles. The influence of a great teacher like James Bradley Thayer or Felix Frankfurter is hard to overestimate: both men turned out dozens of disciples who have since become leading lawyers, politicians, or, in their turn, teachers of the law. Future judges will come from this group. And the give-and-take debate carried on in the law reviews (of which there are now about a hundred) has stimulated legal thought, opened the way for new ideas, and provided a platform through which a writer can reach the entire bench and bar. The better law reviews have opened their columns to political science, economics, sociology, and psychology, thus broadening the approach to modern law.

At the same time it seems likely that the weight of the individual lawyer in federal practice has diminished. Briefs are now often institutional products, and oral argument is usually limited in time.

One may sum up the role of the legal profession by saying that it takes the dominant ideas and philosophy of the day, or of the group which the lawyer represents, and translates these into legal terms acceptable to courts, as Campbell and Choate took the ideology of laissez-faire economics and converted it into the legal doctrines of substantive due process and liberty of contract. Since most lawyers receive the bulk of their incomes from business clients, it is not particularly surprising that the ideas thus presented have frequently been those of the business community. But with the rise of the labor lawyer, the government lawyer, and the legal staffs of various liberal groups like the American Civil Liberties Union and the NAACP, this conservative dominance is certainly not as great as it once was.

Suggestions for Further Reading

Judicial Review as Politics

There are, of course, many writings which take a frankly political approach to judicial review; they cannot all be cited here. Perhaps of most interest would be the following: Fred V. Cahill, *Judicial Legislation* (New York: Ronald Press, 1952); John P. Frank, *Marble Palace* (New York: Alfred A. Knopf, 1958); Alpheus T. Mason, *The Supreme Court: Vehicle of Revealed Truth or Power Group?* (Boston: Boston University Press, 1953); Jack Peltason, *Federal Courts in the Political Process* (Garden City: Doubleday & Co., 1955); Victor G. Rosenblum, *Law as a Political Instrument* (Garden City: Doubleday & Co., 1955); and Herbert Wechsler, *Principles, Politics, and Fundamental Law* (Cambridge: Harvard University Press, 1961).

Statutory Interpretation by Courts

Most of the literature specifically on this question is periodical writing, of which the following are illustrative.

Beaney, William. "Civil Liberties and Statutory Construction," 8 *Jnl. Public Law* 66 (1959).

Beth, Loren P. "Essentiality to Production for Commerce: A Case Study in Statutory Interpretation," 20 *Missouri Law Rev.* 256 (1955).

Bickel, Alexander M., and Wellington, Harry H. "The Legislative Purpose and the Judicial Process," 71 *Harvard Law Rev.* 1 (1957).

Judicial Control of Administrative Agencies

The issues involved here are canvassed succinctly in J. Roland Pennock, *Administration and the Rule of Law* (New York: Farrar & Rinehart, 1941) and in most administrative law texts. The following articles would also provide an introduction to the subject.

Isaacs, Nathan. "Judicial Review of Administrative Findings," 30 *Yale Law Jnl.* 781 (1921).

Jaffe, Louis L. "The Right to Judicial Review in Administrative Law," 71 *Harvard Law Rev.* 401, 769 (1958).

Kramer, Robert. "The Place and Function of Judicial Review in the Administrative Process," 28 *Fordham Law Rev.* 1 (1959).

Judicial Review of State Governmental Action

Any book which discusses judicial review will necessarily spend a good deal of space on this aspect of it; see particularly the works cited for Chapters VII and VIII. A few sources centering especially on the problem may be mentioned here, such as Walter V. Schaefer, *Courts and the Commonplaces of Federalism* (Univ. of Illinois Bulletin, Vol. 56, No. 69, May, 1959); and John R. Schmidhauser, *The Supreme Court as Final Arbiter of Federal-State Relations* (Chapel Hill: University of North Carolina Press, 1958). The following articles are also useful:

Fairman, Charles. "The Supreme Court and the Constitutional Limitations on State Government Authority," 21 *Univ. of Chicago Law Rev.* 40 (1953).

Freund, Paul. "Umpiring the Federal System," 54 *Columbia Law Rev.* 561 (1954).

Wechsler, Herbert. "The Political Safeguards of Federalism," 54 *Columbia Law Rev.* 543 (1954).

Special Supplement: "The Supreme Court and Federalism," *Univ. of Chicago Law School Record*, Vol. 8, No. 1 (1958).

Judicial Review of Actions by Lower Courts

Rather little work has been done in this area, but see Jack W. Peltason, *Fifty-Eight Lonely Men: Southern Federal Judges and School Desegregation* (New York: Harcourt, Brace & World, 1961), and the following articles:

Murphy, Walter F. "Lower Court Checks on Supreme Court Power," 53 *Amer. Pol. Sci. Rev.* 1017 (1959).

Steamer, Robert J. "The Role of the Federal District Courts in the Segregation Controversy," 22 *Jnl. of Politics* 417 (1960).

Note: "Evasion of Supreme Court Mandates in Cases Remanded to State Courts since 1941," 67 *Harvard Law Rev.* 1251 (1954).

Pressure Groups and the Supreme Court

Only in recent years has much study gone into interest groups and their approach to courts. The early work on the subject was Benjamin Twiss's fascinating *Lawyers and the Constitution* (Princeton: Princeton University Press, 1942), which dealt with the role of corporation lawyers in developing the concept of substantive due process. More recently, Clement R. Vose's studies of the NAACP have been of great interest; see his *Caucasians Only* (Berkeley: University of California Press, 1959), and "NAACP Strategy in the Covenant Cases," 6 *Western Reserve Law Rev.* 101 (1955). See also Arnold M. Paul, *Conservative Crisis and the Rule of Law* (Ithaca, N.Y.: Cornell University Press, 1960); Walton H. Hamilton, "The Path of Due Process of Law," in Conyers Read (ed.), *The Constitution Reconsidered* (New York: Columbia University Press, 1938); and, in general, David B. Truman, *The Governmental Process* (New York: Alfred A. Knopf, 1951).

Discretion and Policy Making by the Courts

Almost all modern writings on the Court stress the element of discretion involved in judicial decision making; the references are collected in the notes following Chapter VIII.

Lawyers and the Courts

Here the writings cited just above, by Twiss, Paul, and Hamilton, are of central importance. See also the following articles:

Doro, Marion E. "The Brandeis Brief," 11 *Vanderbilt Law Rev.* 783 (1958).

Harlan, John M. "What Part Does the Oral Argument Play in the Conduct of an Appeal?" 41 *Cornell Law Qtrly.* 6 (1955).

Krastin, Karl. "The Lawyer in Society," 8 *Western Reserve Law Rev.* 409 (1957).

Newland, Chester A. "Legal Periodicals and the United States Supreme Court," 7 *Kansas Law Rev.* 477 (1959).

Symposium: "The Lawyer's Role in Modern Society," 4 *Jnl. Public Law* 1 (1955).

CHAPTER V

The Courts as
Political Agents:
Further Considerations

The greatest judge is one who might have been great in politics, in administration, in business, or in war. Which is simply to say that a great judge must be also a great man.

—JOHN BUCHAN, *Homilies and Recreations*

The Limitations on Judicial Review

The discretionary role of the judge has been, perhaps, overstressed in the preceding chapter—a deliberate device to redress the balance of the common public view of the judiciary. But a judge is not a free agent. While there are alternatives among which he may choose, these are never unlimited, and many of them are, in any practical sense, impossible. No judge in 1879—or even today—could uphold the right of Mormons to maintain polygamy. This is not because polygamy is constitutionally indefensible, but because social beliefs and political factors leave the courts no alternative, whatever the legal situation.

For this reason it is worth a closer look to find just what kinds of limits there are on judicial discretion (and thus on judicial review), how far these limits are effective, and how they affect the institution we call judicial review.

The Constitution

The most obvious—but in some ways the most illusory—limitation is the Constitution itself. Obvious, because if the courts are given the duty of upholding the Constitution against the encroachments of other governmental agencies, the standard must be the Constitution itself. Illusory, because the Constitution's very vagueness is what makes judicial review important.

In any case, all constitutional law must by definition be tied to the Constitution more or less specifically. There have been in the past, it is true, a few cases decided on the basis of "the spirit of our free institutions" [1]—or natural law—and today in the due process field a powerful legal group believes in applying what it calls "the essentials of ordered liberty" to trial procedures.[2] Nevertheless, such instances are exceptional, partly because the appeal to extraconstitutional sources of law is generally unnecessary: the Constitution is capacious enough to incorporate by interpretation most of what we might reasonably wish to include in it.

The Constitution also provides for amendment, and of course amendment constitutes the ultimate limit to the power of the courts. This may be taken in two ways: first, in the sense that the powers of the courts themselves could be directly curbed by restrictive amendments—for instance an amendment prohibiting the exercise of judicial review, or one allowing it only with an extraordinary court majority. Such amendments have been proposed from time to time but have never been seriously considered. Second and more important have been amendments that had the effect of reversing particular decisions of the Supreme Court, of which there are three major examples: the Eleventh Amendment, which prohibits a citizen of one state from suing another state;[3] the Fourteenth, which by its citizenship clause reverses the Dred Scott decision;[4] and the Sixteenth, which permits a federal income tax not uniformly apportioned among the states.[5]

The major problem in connection with a constitutional amending clause, of course, is one of balance. An amendment is a constituent act of the people as a whole. As such it cannot be too easy to use or it will degenerate into popular legislation, thus losing its fundamental character and depriving it of the prolonged and mature public consideration which it deserves. On the other hand, if the process is made too difficult it encourages evasion or frequent new constitutions, as is

---

[1] For instance, Chief Justice John Marshall in *Fletcher* v. *Peck*, 6 Cranch 87 (1810).

[2] The phrase originated with Justice Benjamin Cardozo in *Palko* v. *Connecticut*, 302 U.S. 319 (1937).

[3] A response to the Court's decision in *Chisholm* v. *Georgia*, 2 Dallas 419 (1793).

[4] *Scott* v. *Sandford*, 19 Howard 393 (1857).

[5] A response to *Pollock* v. *Farmers' Loan & Trust Co.*, 158 U.S. 601 (1895).

illustrated in some of our states; this has the effect of reducing popular respect for the document. If the constitution with an excessively difficult amending process is strictly enforced, its life is likely to be concluded by revolt.

The length of life of a constitution is probably the only index to the efficacy of its amending clause, and even this is a far from reliable guide due to the presence of many other factors, such as political stability or the generality of terms in which the constitution is written. Since longevity is a test, the American Constitution—the oldest written national constitution in the world still in active service—would seem to have met it.

In any case, the point to be emphasized here is that the amending clause provides a means by which court decisions may be controlled by reversal, if there is a solid and prolonged public opinion on the question.

The Case System and the Rule of Precedent

A second type of limitation arises from the nature of Anglo-American legal processes. The courts are assumed to handle only properly presented "cases" (which present, presumably, real legal disputes for settlement), and when these cases are decided they are supposed to constitute precedents for the decision of later cases. A more detailed discussion of the workings of the case system and the rule of precedent has already been given. Here, the objective is to assess their significance in setting limits to judicial discretion.

The limiting effect of the case system is obvious, if again somewhat illusory. It accounts for the generally passive role of courts in policy making: they cannot reach out to solve problems, but must wait until the problems are brought to them. The consequences lie in the possibility that some questions will never find their way to the courts, and that others may get there only after the problem has lost its urgency. The Alien and Sedition Acts of 1798 never reached the courts on constitutional grounds, and the Missouri Compromise Act of 1820 did not reach the courts until it had been superseded by later legislation;[6] while the National Industrial Recovery Act of 1933 was invalidated by the Supreme Court some time after its practical effectiveness had reached the vanishing point anyway—or as one wag remarked about this "sick chicken" case, the Supreme Court courageously killed a chicken that was already deathly ill.[7]

Yet it should be recalled that the legal mind has proved remarkably fertile in discovering means by which to construct cases where seemingly none exist: the stockholder's suit is a prime illustration. Given a grievance and a smart lawyer, no one can easily be barred from court

[6] In *Scott* v. *Sandford, supra.*
[7] In *Schechter Poultry Corp.* v. *United States,* 295 U.S. 495 (1935).

action. Reaching the Supreme Court itself is, it is true, somewhat more difficult, since that court can select its own cases to a large extent; but in most instances it is not really necessary to reach the highest court anyway.

As for the rule of precedent, its value as a limitation is restricted primarily to the lower courts, which are bound to follow the decisions of higher courts. Courts of equal rank need not follow each other, nor need they even follow their own precedents. The acceptance of a precedent by the Supreme Court means practically nothing more than that the present justices agree with the earlier decision, either for reasons of desire or of prudence. Prudential considerations may be of great weight since it may sometimes be completely impractical to overturn a line of precedents even though the judge might privately wish to do so. The value of precedent in a legal system has already been considered; the concern at this point is with its effectiveness as a limitation of judicial discretion.

Even more significant than the foregoing in restricting the usefulness of precedent is the fact that the precedents themselves, like the Constitution, are subject to varying interpretations. Two judges using the same set of precedents are thus very likely to arrive at radically differing decisions, yet both can claim they are abiding by the precedents. Then too, the precedents themselves are often conflicting. And, of special importance in constitutional cases, the great history-making decisions are likely to concern new questions, which must therefore be considered without benefit of precedent.

Still, it would be unrealistic to write off the rule of precedent as of only minor significance. For one thing, since the Supreme Court can handle only a few cases, precedent is important as a guide to the lower courts. And despite what has been said above, precedents are often followed, and if law exists even partially to ensure stability and predictability in society, this must be so. This is possibly what Justice Brandeis had in mind when he remarked that while following precedent was not necessary, it was "usually the wise policy."

The Institutionalization of the Judicial Function

The individual judge comes to the bench, as we have seen, with his own ideas of legal philosophy and constitutional law, his own economic and political theory. He soon finds, however, that he is compelled at times to subordinate these to other considerations. He finds, for instance, that he has become (at the appellate level) a member of a collegial body, and he must make his peace with the other members in some fashion if his court is to operate efficiently, harmoniously, and effectively. He finds also that he has joined a body that is the modern representative of an ancient and ongoing tradition that cannot be changed overnight, and will not change drastically even over long periods of time: judges have their own "Hippocratic oath." The personality of the individual, in other words, is inevitably, though only partially, submerged in the institution. The methods of operation, the code of ethics, even the seemingly insignificant customs —all combine to bind him into the institution. He realizes that the court will endure after he is gone just as it has before his presence on it. Its tradition goes back to the Middle Ages. It speaks with the voice of those long gone—Coke, Blackstone, Marshall—and in terms of immutable justice.

Little wonder, then, that few judges become famous as individuals, or live in history books; when history reports their acts it usually does so in the name of the courts, not that of individuals. The wonder, perhaps, is that any judges are strong enough to make their marks as personalities. Yet some have done so, usually when peculiar circumstances combine—a strong man plus a situation where new doctrine is called for, the kind of circumstances existing when John Marshall came to the Supreme Court. At times, too, an individual will stand out because of the comparative mediocrity of his colleagues, as did Oliver Wendell Holmes for some few years after his appointment.

The effect of this institutionalized and venerable college of judges on the freedom of choice of individuals is, of course, intangible and unmeasurable. But even strong and realistic jurists like Benjamin Cardozo have recognized its importance.

Closely associated with the foregoing is the feeling for the law which becomes a part of the nature of every good jurist. Some have it before they finish law school, others acquire it only gradually; many judges never gain it. By "feeling for the law" is meant recognition of the essential role of law in society, and an affection—nay, even a reverence—for the ancient forms of justice through which the law speaks. Justice Robert H. Jackson, quoted in Chapter IV, spoke of the necessity of "a real respect and aspiration for law." Few judges who remain long on the bench escape this attachment wholly; in the great judges of Anglo-American history it has been an almost religious feeling. It tends to make even the most radical man somewhat conservative, at least when his "feeling for the law" becomes involved in a particular case. Even Justices Frank Murphy and William O. Douglas could quote English common law with a relish.

Summing up this consideration, the conclusion seems to be that a judge cannot always do as he pleases: the pressure of tradition, of his colleagues, of the very objectives of a legal system, often push and pull him whither he might not freely go.

The Lack of Enforcement Powers

"John Marshall has made his decision, now let him enforce it." President Andrew Jackson is said to have challenged the Supreme

Court in these words.[8] Whether Jackson ever made such a remark is problematical, but he could realistically have done so, for an outstanding fact about the courts is that they do not have the power to enforce their own decisions: they can "say something. The effect depends on others." All enforcement is in the hands of the very agencies of government that the courts may be trying to check—the federal or the state executive or legislature. This means that the courts must be careful not to make decisions that will not be enforced, for to do so would be to destroy themselves. The doctrine of political questions was developed as a means of avoiding such decisions, but in many cases a decision cannot be avoided, and the better part of wisdom may be to accede to the government's position. Striking examples both of evasion and of the consequences of the refusal to evade are provided by the conduct of Chief Justice Roger B. Taney on the Maryland circuit during the Civil War. In Ex parte Merryman Taney issued a writ of habeas corpus to free Merryman from military detention, but the military authorities refused to accede to the writ or even to appear in court to show cause why they should not do so. The result was a blow to the power of the courts, even though Taney's vehement written opinion is considered an important civil liberties document.[9]

Having apparently learned his lesson, Taney avoided further brushes with the military. In the treason cases arising out of the war, he postponed hearings indefinitely, writing to Justice Samuel Nelson that he did so because if the defendants were tried fairly—which seemed unlikely—and freed, the military would refuse to obey the writs anyway. He feared that such an eventuality would contribute to the degradation of the court system. This is an extreme instance, and it must be admitted that respect for the courts is likely to decline just as much when they refuse to decide legitimate cases as when they decide them in an unenforceable manner.

Particularly perplexing problems are presented to the courts when social problems of a sectional nature must be decided. In the School Segregation Cases the Court has apparently expressed an opinion acceptable to most Americans, but not to most white Southerners. Since the decision cannot be enforced by the Court, nor even (realistically) by the federal government itself, but mainly by state and local authorities, the difficulties in the way of enforcement of the decision are numerous.[10] Whether the prestige of the Supreme Court is by itself great enough to ensure eventual compliance is still problematical. The question then becomes, aside from the constitutional and humanitarian arguments, should the Court make such a decision?

---

[8] In reaction to the Court's decision in Worcester v. Georgia, 6 Peters 515 (1832).

[9] Ex parte Merryman, Fed. Case 9487 (1861).

[10] Brown v. Board of Education, 347 U.S. 483 (1954), and 349 U.S. 294 (1955).

Self-imposed Limitations

"The only restraint on the courts," wrote Justice Harlan Stone, "is our own sense of self-restraint." While as we have seen this is not literally true, it does contain a large measure of truth. Some of the points already discussed illustrate it; they add up to a sense of judicial ethics reinforced by a lively appreciation of political and social realities. Several other devices of self-restraint may be mentioned.

The *doctrine of political questions* has been referred to at several points earlier. In substance, it is the idea that some questions can only properly be decided by the "political" branches of the government. This doctrine was first made explicit when the Supreme Court refused to intervene in a dispute as to the legal government of Rhode Island in the 1840's.[11] It has been used with some frequency throughout our history. The legal justification for the doctrine seems quite dubious; the Constitution sets no boundaries between "political" and "legal" questions, nor can the two be separated logically. Consequently the doctrine of political questions must be regarded as a counsel of judicial prudence—keep your fingers out of places where they may get pinched—rather than as a real "constitutional" doctrine. It expresses the judges' conviction that they have no particular competence to decide, that they could not enforce a decision if made, or, most likely, a vague feeling that the courts should not meddle in the particular kind of question involved in the case. Thus the courts may refuse to decide some questions even though a real "case" is presented.

It should be noted, however, that even a refusal to rule amounts to a ruling, for in most instances the judges know perfectly well what decision the "political" authorities will reach. Refusal to decide thus becomes a sort of silent acquiescence, and in a moral sense the courts may be as responsible for the decision as if they had made it themselves.

Another self-restraint doctrine is the *presumption of constitutionality*. This means that the courts will place the burden of proof on the challenger: an act of government will be considered constitutional unless proven otherwise to the satisfaction of the court. Or to phrase it differently, any doubts will be resolved in favor of the government. The doctrine in its literal sense is often mentioned but seldom used, for reasons which should be apparent. If a law were of undoubted constitutionality, it would not likely be challenged in court; if it were beyond question *un*constitutional, it would probably not have been enacted. Therefore most constitutional cases coming to the courts present questions the answers to which are uncertain, and strict following of the doctrine would mean that judicial review would be of extremely limited applicability, since the courts would be obligated to uphold almost all laws. Obviously the doctrine has not been used in this

---

[11] *Luther v. Borden*, 7 Howard 1 (1849).

sense; what it does seem to mean is that there is no doubt of the measure's unconstitutionality in the mind of the *individual* judge: if there were, he would vote to uphold it. It does not mean that there is no question in the court as a whole, as frequent divided votes eloquently testify.

On the whole, then, it is dubious whether the presumption of constitutionality operates as a real restraint. Many of the judges who have cited it most often have been at the same time quite active in findings of unconstitutionality. Yet they were clearly sincere in their protestations that they were applying the presumption: there actually *was* no doubt in their minds.

A final self-restraint device is the denial of *certiorari*. The writ of certiorari, at this point, may be regarded merely as a legal device which enables the Supreme Court largely to decide for itself which cases it will hear and which ones will be finally decided by the circuit courts of appeals or the state courts. In one form or another this has long been possible, but since the 1920's Congress has broadened the power's scope so that the writ is now used in about 90 per cent of the cases reaching the Supreme Court. In recent years the Court has accepted only about two hundred cases each year. Clearly there is a good deal of winnowing done. Since the use of certiorari has been discussed earlier, suffice it to point out here that the Court may deliberately refuse to accept cases in order to avoid ruling on the questions they present. Of course, the lower courts must rule anyway; the utility of the device is that the Supreme Court can postpone decision until a later date, when political passions have subsided or public or legal opinion has solidified so that a more realistic decision may be reached. If the question is a significant one or one in which national uniformity is desirable, certiorari must eventually be granted.

Summing up the matter of self-restraint, it should be noted that its use has varied a great deal in different periods of our history. Courts before the Civil War and since 1937 have exercised a great deal of restraint, while the period from 1870 to 1937 became notorious for its relatively unrestrained play of judicial discretion. This is apparently a product of the times and the men. The great change in the ideas of the proper role of government in society which came gradually after the Civil War combined with the natural conservatism of the bench to produce courts that were reluctant to accept the change and that exerted their power to prevent it. But over the long run of our history the courts have seemed to feel that their power is greatest when it is used with moderation.

Public Opinion

De Tocqueville long ago pointed out the importance of public opinion in guiding the courts, in the following words:

. . . Their power is enormous, but it is the power of public opinion. They are all-powerful as long as the people respect the law, but they would be impotent against popular neglect or contempt of the law. The force of public opinion is the most intractable of agents, because its exact limits cannot be defined; and it is not less dangerous to exceed than to remain below the boundary prescribed.[12]

Less accurately but more pungently the political humorist Mr. Dooley observed that "th' Supreme Court follows th' iliction returns."

So much has already been said, and will be said, in this book about the power of public opinion that little needs to be added here. Over the years it has become obvious that the course of court decision has, in general, been parallel to the major trends in American thought. Commentators, historians, and judges themselves have become very much aware of this fact; so much so that into some recent judicial opinions has even crept a rather vague feeling that the Supreme Court ought consciously to look at the state of public opinion in a deliberate effort to keep in step. Such a course, however, is not necessary to vindicate De Tocqueville's insight, and many observers feel that its use would destroy judicial review, for we assume that our "popular" branches of government sufficiently represent public opinion, and, we have seen, the courts were intentionally insulated from the public. This insulation does not make them impervious to major trends in popular thought, but it may enable them to separate temporary desires from semipermanent ideals and aspirations, preserving the latter while refusing to allow the former where they clash with constitutional dictates.

Congressional Controls

An element in the limitation of the courts which is often lost sight of, but which is of tremendous importance, is the possibility of legislation passed by Congress to curb the courts. A great deal of the actual power of the federal courts, even that of the constitutionally created Supreme Court, is held only on the sufferance of the legislative branch. It is thus extremely significant that Congress has never passed laws drastically curbing the judicial power, but on the contrary has enlarged its scope—and doubtless this one fact illustrates sufficiently the strength of the general support of Americans for the "rule of law" as we know it.

What Congressional control adds up to is this: that if the courts ever completely blocked the public will they would run the risk of reprisal at the hands of the people's representatives in the legislature. And short of amending the Constitution there are several powerful deterrents which can be applied by Congress.

---

[12] Alexis de Tocqueville, *Democracy in America* (New York: Vintage Books, 1954), Vol. I, p. 157.

First, there is the possibility of evasive action: getting around a court ruling by trying to reach the same objective in a different way. The possibilities here are endless, given a real determination and a solid backing by the public. If a processing tax is an unconstitutional means of aiding farmers, use conservation benefits instead;[13] if a regulation of child labor is invalid under the commerce power, try the taxing power;[14] if segregation is not allowed in public facilities, convert them to private use.[15]

There is, however, one principal difficulty. Evasive methods are quite often more cumbersome and less satisfactory than the original. As a consequence they may be impractical. (Are private schools in the South an acceptable substitute for the public school system?) It is possible, too, that the evasion may be adjudged unconstitutional, as happened in the case of child labor legislation. Nevertheless, if the will is there Congress (or the state legislature) is likely, eventually, to have its way; where the courts have won, it has usually been because the matter has been of transitory or historical interest and Congress has lost its will.

A second weapon possessed by Congress is the power to change the structure of the federal courts. At its extreme this could mean the abolition of all federal courts except the Supreme Court itself. On a less drastic scale, the use of terms of office, elections, or presidential or legislative removal from office for federal judges below the Supreme Court would be of tremendous impact on the court system. The Supreme Court cannot constitutionally be abolished, nor can the life tenure of its members be interfered with. But even here the several court-packing schemes—successful and unsuccessful—have been motivated by the desire to control the Court. A glance at Civil War and reconstruction history is enough to prove the point.

At the outbreak of hostilities the Supreme Court consisted of nine members, but in early 1863 a tenth position was added in order to create a far western circuit, and Stephen J. Field of California was appointed. The clear purpose was to help cement the ties of political loyalty, so that California would support the Union cause.

After Lincoln's assassination and the war's end, both the new president—Andrew Johnson—and the Supreme Court fell into disfavor with the radical Republicans who controlled Congress and espoused a "tough" peace policy. In order to prevent Johnson from appointing "moderates" to the Court, Congress reduced the membership

---

[13] As Congress did to evade the Court's holding in *United States* v. *Butler*, 297 U.S. 1 (1936).

[14] Congress' response to *Hammer* v. *Dagenhart*, 247 U.S. 251 (1918); unfortunately, the tax was also found unconstitutional in *Bailey* v. *Drexel Furniture Co.*, 259 U.S. 20 (1922). Federal child labor laws were finally judicially upheld in *United States* v. *Darby Lumber Co.*, 312 U.S. 100 (1941).

[15] As many Southern states have tried to do since *Brown* v. *Board of Education*, 347 U.S. 483 (1954).

to *seven*. Consequently when Justices John Catron and James M. Wayne died they could not be replaced, so that by the end of Johnson's presidency only eight judges were sitting.

With Johnson out of the way there remained no reason for a seven-man Court; with the war ended there was no further need for catering particularly to the far west; and with the election of Ulysses S. Grant, a stalwart Republican, there was a desire to give him the opportunity to appoint as many other faithful party men as possible to federal jobs. So the Court's size was restored to its prewar nine, and Grant made good use of the extra appointment as a means of ensuring the reversal of the first *Legal Tender Case*.[16]

Still a third means by which Congress may limit the courts is by the manipulation of their jurisdictions. Certain parts, though not necessarily the most important, of the Supreme Court's jurisdiction are constitutionally defined, but outside this limited area Congress could probably take the Court's jurisdiction and bestow it anywhere or nowhere. Even though the power of judicial review would remain, there would likely be few cases to which it could apply. This statement applies to the appellate jurisdiction of the Court with particular force.[17]

It requires no great amount of analysis to decide why few of these things have been done by Congress. Two reasons stand out: first, the advantages to be gained from an orderly, known, and stable legal system are too vital to be tampered with except for serious and prolonged cause. Second, the attachment of our people to an independent and powerful judiciary has made it impossible—usually even inconceivable—that any drastic changes will be made except in abnormally confused periods.

The limitations on judicial power, surveyed above, are many and varied. It can be seen that the discretionary power of judges is by no means unconfined. Nevertheless their power remains great—great enough to make it important for us to take a further look at the decision-making process and at the judge as an individual—at how he arrives on the bench and how, as an individual, he influences its work.

Grounds for Judicial Decision

The fact that American courts at the appellate level are required to write opinions justifying their decisions means that judges must find reasons. While as this text has stressed, most constitutional decisions

---

[16] The first legal tender case, *Hepburn* v. *Griswold*, 8 Wallace 603 (1870), was reversed in *Knox* v. *Lee*, 12 Wallace 457 (1871).

[17] The major instance is Congress' withdrawal from the Court of jurisdiction in cases arising under the Habeas Corpus Act of 1867. The action was taken to prevent the Court from ruling in *Ex parte McCardle*, 7 Wallace 506 (1869).

are political in nature, and while the emotions, convictions, and prejudices of judges play an important part in decision making, the legal context in which the process takes place requires that political and personal elements cannot be too openly admitted as the reasons for decision. Wisely, the system of written opinions forces the judge to search for other reasons than his own preferences—in other words, he is forced to *rationalize* his decision. The possibility (even probability) of dissent and public criticism requires him to do the best he can in the rationalizing process.

In studying court decisions it is necessary for the student to keep two major questions in mind: first, what are the given reasons for the decision; and second, are the given reasons the real ones? Such an approach requires of the student a good deal of discrimination and sophistication, but only such a twofold approach can provide a thorough understanding.

A complicating factor is presented by the fact that the grounds given for decision are generally multiple: no lawyer is satisfied with one reason if he can think of two. Therefore many cases will present several reasons for the decision; among them some may be more important than others—perhaps even the real reason will be found among them!

Several of the grounds commonly used have already been surveyed in other connections. Among these are the use of the standing to sue and case or controversy rules as justifications for avoiding decision. The doctrine of political questions falls in the same category, and the rule of precedent has also been previously discussed. Briefly, other grounds often used for decision will now be surveyed.

Plain and Implied Meaning

Possibly the most often mentioned but least often used of legal grounds for decision is the plain meaning of the constitutional text. It is a deceptively simple method; in essence all it involves is the use of a dictionary. But, as Justice Robert H. Jackson points out, if the text "makes the answer clear, there is no problem. It is the imprecise, obscure or ambiguous state of the text that raises the issue."

If the meaning of a constitutional clause is clear, there will be little or no litigation involving its interpretation. On the other hand, if it is not clear, there is no plain meaning to apply. Most words have several proper uses; sometimes the same word may mean different things depending on whether its ordinary or its technical usage is relied upon. For these reasons, although judges often cite the plain meaning rule, dissenters are likely to point out that the meaning is not plain to them; actually what is being done by the majority in such cases is to fill in the meaning out of the assumptions and preconceptions of the judges.

A further serious problem with the use of plain meaning is that the meaning of words and phrases changes with changing times. Should a phrase be interpreted for all time as fixed in meaning? Or should the changing meaning be used by courts as an adaptive device to elasticize constitutional interpretation? Professor W. W. Crosskey has argued powerfully that the words of the Constitution should always be interpreted in the light of their commonly accepted meaning when written.[18] The difficulties accompanying the use of this method, however, are so numerous and serious as to make it seem impracticable. If we concede that many words have, at any point in time, several correct meanings, it becomes difficult to pick out the one the framers meant to use. When one or two hundred years lie between the writing and the interpretation, troubles multiply, for one cannot even be certain that he has found all of the possible correct meanings, much less that he has divined the one the framers intended.

On the other hand, changing the meaning has its own difficulties. It deprives the law of some of its certainty. And it depends perhaps too greatly on the chance element: five justices who "happen" to be on the Supreme Court bench can change the meaning of the Constitution to suit their ideas of its "proper" contemporary meaning.

Most of the time, words do not have genuinely plain meanings if they are subject to much litigation. It is well in this connection to remember that our Constitution in many of its parts was written in generalities. This is particularly true of the power-granting sections. Consequently, it is usually necessary for the courts to decide the meaning of a phrase in the absence of any known commonly accepted meaning. It will readily be understood that this is true of the Commerce Clause, for instance. But it also applies to many other clauses.

The use of implied meaning has often been cited by constitutional scholars as the principal method by which a written constitution with a difficult amending process may be adapted to the needs of a changing society. While its importance in this connection is difficult to overestimate, the opportunities for the exercise of a "wise discretion" in constitutional interpretation are so numerous that a great deal of constitutional adaptation by the courts may actually take place without the use of implied meanings.

The Intentions of the Framers

Often the Court will try to figure out just what the framers of the Constitution or its amendments were trying to do. Early cases, while the framers were still living, would naturally exhibit this method most often, but it is still used today with surprising frequency. The object

---

[18] W. W. Crosskey, *Politics and the Constitution in the History of the United States* (Chicago: University of Chicago Press, 1953), Vol. I.

of the method is, of course, to carry out the intentions of those who wrote the Constitution. If such intentions could be clearly known, and if this method was used rigidly, it would result in an inflexible Constitution. The life of the Constitution has been lengthened indefinitely by the fortunate facts that the Court often does not seem to care what the framers wanted, and that even if it does care it is impossible to be sure what they did want, particularly when clauses must be applied to circumstances unforeseen at the time they were written.

If, as in the *Slaughterhouse Cases*,[19] the Court uses the plain meaning approach, this makes it impossible to use the framers' intentions; and which approach is used is likely to be decided subconsciously on the basis of what decision is desired. Both methods involve the filling of a partial vacuum with the preconceptions of individual judges. In the *New Jersey School Bus Case*, for instance, in which the Court tried to figure out what the framers meant to do in reference to public aid to religion, the uncertainty of the framers' intent is clear: there were few if any public schools in 1789, no school busses, etc.: how then could their intent (even if known) apply to the present situation? It is obvious that Justice Hugo Black and the majority were actually trying to figure out what the framers would say if they were alive today, not what they said in 1789—but this is tantamount to deciding on the basis of what Justice Black *thinks* they would say, which is very difficult to separate from what he thinks they ought to say.[20]

Conservatives may use the intentions of the framers to prevent change and adaptation. Justice George Sutherland once said, for instance:

> A provision of the Constitution, it is hardly necessary to say, does not admit of two distinctly opposite interpretations. It does not mean one thing at one time and an entirely different thing at another time. . . . The whole aim of construction, as applied to a provision of the Constitution, is to discover the meaning, ascertain and give effect to the intent, of its framers and the people who adopted it. . . .[21]

Sutherland's views imply that present opinion should be abandoned for that of the framers, and that the meaning of the Constitution is changeless. But even were this theoretically desirable, the attempt to discover intent is futile, and the result is, once more, that the judge is likely to "discover" the intention which *he* would approve.

---

[19] *Slaughterhouse Cases*, 16 Wallace 36 (1873).
[20] *Everson* v. *Board of Education*, 330 U.S. 1 (1947).
[21] Dissenting in *Home Building & Loan Association* v. *Blaisdell*, 290 U.S. 398 (1934).

Policy Considerations

Due to the legal context in which courts operate, policy premises for decision (while, as we have shown earlier, are often present) must usually be implicit rather than overt. The courts cannot publicly admit that they are deciding on political rather than legal grounds. Yet frequently decisions have taken into account the effects they will have on the economic, social, or political welfare of the nation. Chief Justice Roger B. Taney was quite explicit when, in the *Charles River Bridge Case*, he asked:

If this Court should establish the principles now contended for, what is to become of the numerous railroads established on the same line of travel with turnpike companies . . . ? . . . We shall be thrown back to the improvements of the last century, and obliged to stand still until the claims of the old turnpike corporations shall be satisfied. . . . Nor is this all. This Court will find itself compelled to fix, by some arbitrary rule, the width of this new kind of property in a line of travel. . . . This Court are not prepared to sanction principles which must lead to such results.[22]

It is the knowledge of considerations such as these which led Justice Oliver Wendell Holmes to remark:

The very considerations which judges most rarely mention, and always with an apology, are the secret root from which the law draws all the juices of life. I mean, of course, considerations of what is expedient for the community concerned.[23]

One should not become too cynical about the hypocrisy contained in such judicial action, for after all, judges are Americans desirous of furthering the welfare of their country like other citizens; and in addition, the impossibility of separating one's judgment of what is *good* from one's judgment of what is *constitutional* poses a problem for a Solomon. Yet a judge is hardly in a position, as a member of our highest legal institution, to take a forthright stand on the political, economic, or social merits of an issue; as a judge he is more or less bound to wrap his judgments in legal phraseology. The hypocrisy involved is thus not intentional but forced. Further, the fact that he must find good legal reasons for his opinions probably makes for wiser decisions in the long run.

The Limits on Judicial Competence

Not infrequently the Supreme Court will be faced with a question that for some reason it does not feel that it can decide. But if it

---

[22] *Charles River Bridge* v. *Warren Bridge*, 11 Peters 420 (1837).
[23] Oliver Wendell Holmes, Jr., *The Common Law* (Boston: Little, Brown & Co., 1881), p. 35.

has a case before it, how can it refuse to make a decision? To handle some cases of this nature the Court has developed what may be called the "doctrine of judicial incompetence." The Court in using this doctrine admits that it is not, for any of a number of reasons, qualified to decide the particular case. Probably the most common form of this is the doctrine of political questions, which has already been discussed. The Court says, "This is a question that we are not qualified to decide because its political nature makes it one for the political agencies of government to handle."

Another type of limit sometimes relied upon is the Court's lack of expert knowledge. If the courts feel that they do not have the type of knowledge required to decide a case, they may bow to the decision of the other governmental agency set up to handle such questions. But here again the Court may use its own discretion: it may decide to rule on the case despite its lack of *expertise*. The exchange between Justices Felix Frankfurter and Robert H. Jackson in the two *Flag Salute Cases* illustrates both possibilities. Frankfurter, holding that the state may require a flag salute, said that for the Court to overrule the judgment of state authorities in this field "would amount to no less than the pronouncement of pedagogical and psychological dogma in a field where courts possess no marked and certainly no controlling competence." [24] But two years later when the Court reversed itself, Jackson replied:

. . . Nor does our duty to apply the Bill of Rights to assertions of official authority depend on our possession of marked competence in the field where the invasion of rights occurs. . . . We act in these matters not by authority of our competence but by force of our commissions. We cannot, because of modest estimates of our competence . . . withhold the judgment that history authenticates as the function of this Court when liberty is infringed.[25]

The field of substantive due process is an illustration of the Court's refusal to bow to expert knowledge possessed by other agencies, for often in its use the Court deliberately substituted its judgment in technical questions for the judgments of agencies set up by the states for the specific purpose of developing and using expert knowledge. This is especially true of the rate cases. The Court has often been criticized both by outsiders and by its own members for its refusal in such cases to pay sufficient heed to the findings of expert bodies on questions of rate-fixing and valuation. Thus Justice Black sharply criticized the court majority in his concurring opinion in *Federal Power Commission* v. *Natural Gas Pipeline*.

It is not the function of the courts to prescribe what formula should be used. The fact that one may be fair to investors does not mean that another

---

[24] *Minersville School District* v. *Gobitis*, 310 U.S. 586 (1940).
[25] *West Virginia State Board of Education* v. *Barnette*, 319 U.S. 624 (1943).

would be unfair. The decision in each case must turn on considerations of justness and fairness which cannot be cast into a legalistic formula. The rate of return to be allowed in any given case calls for a highly expert judgment. That judgment has been entrusted to the [Federal Power] Commission. There it should rest.[26]

In recent years, while the Court has not explicitly given up its powers of review in such cases, the power has been exercised in such a way as practically to concede that the determinations of the expert agencies are final. Only in cases exhibiting drastic unfairness would the Court intervene today.

Common Law

While the federal courts have no common-law jurisdiction, nevertheless at times cases arise which make it desirable to know and use common-law principles. This is true because certain common-law concepts and terms appear in the Constitution or in laws passed. Thus, in *Munn* v. *Illinois*, the Court turned to English common-law precedents to prove that governments had always exercised the power to regulate certain businesses, and that the Constitution should thus be assumed to have "imported" this principle from the common law.[27] The common law can thus be used as an aid to constitutional interpretation. It cannot, of course, be controlling, for it is the Constitution which is being interpreted, not the common law. Common-law rules can govern only when the Court can find that they explain the meaning of a relevant part of the Constitution.

Natural Law and Its Variants

The idea of natural law constitutes an appeal to something higher than human will or act—a rule of conduct contained in Nature, or handed down by Divine Will, which is in substance a sort of higher equity principle. Natural-law theories were commonly held before and during the formative period of the United States; it follows that our Constitution not only was an attempt to *state* the laws of nature, but that in a sense natural law was conceived to stand *above* the Constitution. Natural-law philosophy is no longer the vogue today, but there are certain other principles which may be regarded as serving the same purposes.

For a time natural law was regarded as a proper basis for constitutional decision, though it was usually combined with other grounds. In *Fletcher* v. *Peck* Chief Justice John Marshall based his opinion almost exclusively on his doubt "whether the nature of society and

---

[26] *Federal Power Commission* v. *Natural Gas Pipeline Co.*, 315 U.S. 575 (1942).

[27] *Munn* v. *Illinois*, 94 U.S. 113 (1877).

of government does not prescribe some limits to the legislative power"; he concluded that either the Constitution or "the general principles which are common to our free institutions" (he did not specify which) operated to nullify the action of Georgia which was involved in the case. Nevertheless, the fact that he had to mention the Constitution was significant; the finding of principles of natural law is a philosophical, not a judicial, enterprise.[28]

With the decline of the belief in natural law, the courts have not used it in its simple form, but the idea of fundamental principles outside and underlying the Constitution, and sought and found by judges through some mysterious process known only to justices, has reappeared in different forms. One of these is substantive due process. The phrase "due process of law" in its usual common-law meaning required mainly that no one be convicted of a crime without a fair trial. The Supreme Court, however, after 1890 used this phrase as a sort of substitute for natural law in protecting business corporations from regulation by states. This is called "substantive" due process, since it looks to the *substance* of governmental action rather than the procedures used. It amounts to saying that there are some things the states cannot do, not because of any constitutional prohibition, but because it is not right or just. There have been numerous cases in which substantive due process was used, but the theory of right and wrong which it assumes has seldom been made explicit. Justice Stephen J. Field, it is true, said in his *Slaughterhouse* dissent, "grants of exclusive privileges are opposed to the whole theory of free government, and it requires no aid from any bill of rights to render them void," but this was more a statement of natural law than of substantive due process.[29]

Alpheus Mason has remarked that since the concept of substantive due process "provided no 'fixed standard,' all the Court could properly say in raising it as a constitutional bar was that the legislature had passed an act that in the opinion of the judges was inconsistent with abstract principles of justice." [30] The phrase "abstract principles of justice" is an apt description—it is also the statement of a principle of natural law. The essence of natural law is that it is abstract: it does not exist in the written law which the courts presumably are construing.

Though substantive due process as a protection of corporate property is not presently used by the federal courts, a modern variant lives on in the application of the same concept to civil liberties. This variant is sometimes called "the concept of ordered liberty." The due process clause is now used as a means by which courts can apply the protec-

---

[28] See note 1, this chapter.
[29] See note 19, this chapter.
[30] Alpheus T. Mason and William Beaney, *American Constitutional Law* (New York: Prentice-Hall, Inc., 1954), p. 412.

tions of the Bill of Rights to the states through the Fourteenth Amendment, so that state acts infringing free speech or violating fair trial principles may be declared unconstitutional. This in itself would not be relevant to the "natural law" basis for decision, since the Constitution's Bill of Rights is a set of specific provisions, not an abstract principle. But the Court has never admitted that it is applying the *whole* Bill of Rights bodily to the states; as a matter of fact it has specifically many times refused to do so. The question is thus raised, What portions of the Bill of Rights *will* be applied? On what basis can the Court pick and choose among the provisions of the Bill of Rights, and perhaps even add to them? Justice Benjamin Cardozo in discussing this question said that the Court acted on the basis of "a rationalizing principle" which he defined as "the very essence of a scheme of ordered liberty." In substance he seemed to mean that the judges will enforce against the states those principles that they believe are necessary for the maintenance of "ordered liberty." [31] But this can be done only on the basis of some concept in the minds of individual judges, which seems in the final analysis to be the same thing as natural law. Since it is not in the Constitution, it must be graven on the heavens in language which, presumably, only judges can read. The processes of justice in our states, then, must conform to the ideas of at least five men on the Supreme Court, not to explicit constitutional provisions. Justice Black has astutely remarked that such natural-law theories "degrade the constitutional safeguards of the Bill of Rights and simultaneously appropriate for this Court a broad power which we are not authorized by the Constitution to exercise." Black concluded: "Conceding the possibility that this Court is now wise enough to improve on the Bill of Rights by substituting natural-law concepts for . . . [it], I think the possibility is entirely too speculative to agree to take that course." [32]

The Presumption of Constitutionality or Unconstitutionality

The presumption of constitutionality—that a law will not be invalidated by the Court unless it is clearly unconstitutional—has been discussed earlier as a means by which the Court exercises self-restraint. It may be repeated here that it is a doctrine which has been so often disregarded and is so easily liable to misuse that it is practically useless to analyze it. A recent school of thought has proposed reversing the presumption in civil liberties cases, i.e., that the Court assume laws unconstitutional in this area unless the state can prove their

---

[31] See note 2, this chapter.
[32] Dissenting in *Adamson* v. *California*, 332 U.S. 46 (1947).

necessity for some legitimate and basic purpose. Justice Frank Murphy, for instance, thought that the Court should consider any violation of First-Amendment rights as "prima facie invalid." Religious freedom, he believed, "is too sacred a right to be restricted or prohibited in any degree without convincing proof that a legitimate interest of the states is in grave danger." [33] Most of the Court has in recent years accepted this idea to a greater or lesser degree, and nowadays laws that limit First-Amendment freedoms must face a more exacting judicial scrutiny than those in any other field.

The foregoing survey of bases for decision illustrates once again both the wide discretion available to courts and the limitations on that discretion which are imposed by the legal context in which they work. On the whole, one is almost driven to agree with Justice Holmes that "the felt necessities of the times, the prevalent moral and political theories, intuitions of public policy, avowed or unconscious, even the prejudices which judges share with their fellowmen" are more important in judicial decision making than are strictly legal principles; and this seems especially true of decision making in the field of constitutional interpretation. The fact seems to be that there is a wide enough variety of legal bases for decision so that courts and judges can to a significant extent "pick and choose" among them so as to reach a consciously or subconsciously desired result. Again this fact emphasizes the role of discretion and thus the influence of individual judges.

The Selection and Influence of Judges

The most evident point at which partisan politics enters into our legal system is the moment at which a judge *becomes* a judge. For here all the political considerations are more or less out in the open and explicit. It has been many years now since the general public entertained the naïve notion that members of the federal bench were selected with no other consideration than their probable excellence as jurists. And as a matter of fact it is very difficult to predict how able a judge a man *will* be, or even to decide how successful he *has* been! Citizens have an extreme tendency to think a judge is good when he decides in line with their own prejudices, and to regard him as a poor judge if he does not; and this tendency blurs the distinction between the able, the mediocre, and the poor.

For these reasons plus the ones we have already studied—that the courts are a "power center" in the American political system due to the large element of discretion they must exercise—it should at once

---

[33] In *Prince* v. *Massachusetts*, 321 U.S. 158 (1944).

be apparent that the appointment of a new judge to the federal bench is a serious political move, calling for a good deal of political wisdom as well as due concern for the quality of the bench. Some of the considerations which lead to an appointment are fairly obvious, others are not, and some are more obviously political than others. Let us look first at the various factors that are influential in the choice of federal judges, giving most attention to the Supreme Court not only because it is the highest but because we know the most about it.

Political Factors in the Selection of Judges

One of the most significant factors in selection, of course, is party membership and activity, because it constitutes the clearest index of a man's political opinions. From President Washington's day to our own, the large majority of all federal court appointments has been made along strict party lines. This observation is so commonplace that it obscures more than it reveals of the nature of the appointing process. For in the American party system each party contains all sorts of men holding all sorts of opinions. To say that President Kennedy will select a Democrat for the bench tells the hearer almost nothing about the man who will be chosen, for there are conservatives, middle-roaders, liberals, and mavericks in the Democratic party. Also, confining one's observations to the matter of party fails completely to explain why, at times, a President will appoint members of the opposite party. It becomes clear, then, that party membership is not the prime consideration; and even when it is one must look farther to discover why a particular man was appointed.

A second factor, which goes beyond mere party ties, lies in the nature of the President's program. Other considerations aside, there is no doubt that a President will seek a man who will represent on the bench the objectives for which the administration is striving. This thought doubtless lay behind President John Adams' appointment of John Marshall; Jefferson's selection of William Johnson; Lincoln's choice of Salmon P. Chase—to name only a few prominent examples. Rarely, however, has this element in the selection of a judge been made as explicit as it was by "Teddy" Roosevelt. While considering the appointment of Oliver Wendell Holmes, he wrote to Senator Henry Cabot Lodge:

In the ordinary and low sense which we attach to the words "partisan" and "politician," a judge of the Supreme Court should be neither. But in the higher sense, in the proper sense, he is not in my judgement fitted for the position unless he is a party man, a constructive statesman, constantly keeping in mind his adherence to the principles and policies under which this nation has been built up and in accordance with which it must go on; and keeping in mind also his relations with his fellow statesmen who in other branches of the government are striving in cooperation with him to advance the ends of government.

Now I should like to know that Judge Holmes was in entire sympathy with your views and mine . . . before I would feel justified in appointing him. Judge Gray was one of the most valuable members of the Court. I should hold myself as guilty of an irreparable wrong to the nation if I should put in his place any man who was not absolutely sane and sound on the great national policies for which we stand in public life.[34]

Apparently Lodge satisfied the President in this regard, for Holmes was appointed; but he proved to be somewhat of a disappointment to Roosevelt—so much so that for a time, it is said, the President even refused to invite Holmes to the White House!

President William Howard Taft, too, openly (if facetiously) admitted the importance of agreement between courts and administration. When he was defeated for re-election by the liberal Woodrow Wilson in 1912, he said, in reference to the six men he had appointed to the Supreme Court: "And I have said to them . . . 'Damn you, if any of you die, I'll disown you!' "

Many years later, when the aging Taft was Chief Justice, he still clung to the same ideas, except that now he wanted the administration to agree with the courts instead of vice versa. The election of Herbert Hoover to the Presidency in 1928 was, to Taft, a sign of a dangerous radicalism in the United States, and he conceived it to be his duty to outlast Hoover, holding his seat until a safe conservative President could fill the vacancy. He wrote:

I am older and slower and less acute and more confused. However, as long as things continue as they are, and I am able to answer in my place, I must stay on the court in order to prevent the Bolsheviki from getting control. . . .

It need not be emphasized that the considerations expressed by Roosevelt and Taft go far beyond the question of party membership. Taft's promotion of Edward Douglass White, a Democrat, to the Chief Justiceship reinforces the point. White was a Southerner and a conservative, even though a Democrat. His position on issues was of more weight than his party. Since it is sometimes considered important to have all the major geographical regions of the nation represented on the Supreme Court, and it is difficult to find prominent Southern lawyers or politicians who are Republicans, it may be thought necessary for a Republican President to favor a Democrat; but he will be careful to try to find a conservative one.

Nevertheless this does not mean that party is a minor consideration. And it is also true that appointment to judicial posts has often served as a reward for faithful or valuable services to the party (or, perhaps more likely, to the administration), such, for example, as had been rendered by Hugo Black in the early years of the New Deal, or by Earl Warren in the Republican cause. Any judicial post carries with

---

[34] Quoted in Felix Frankfurter, *Mr. Justice Holmes and the Supreme Court* (Cambridge: Harvard University Press, 1938), pp. 21–22.

it a good deal of prestige, and the prestige of a Supreme Court position is second only to that of the Presidency itself. Court appointments have sometimes also been given in order to keep defeated
Congressional candidates in active service; when Sherman Minton was
retired from the Senate by the voters of Indiana, President Franklin
Roosevelt appointed him to the federal bench, from which he was later
elevated to the Supreme Court by President Harry Truman.

Religion has also, in modern times, played a role in court appointments. It has become "customary" to have a Jew and a Catholic on
the Supreme Court. Thus when Justice Benjamin Cardozo died he was
replaced by Justice Felix Frankfurter, another Jew. However, despite
this custom there was no Catholic on the Court from Justice Frank
Murphy's death in 1947 until 1956, which emphasizes the fact that
custom may be broken if there seem to be no compelling reasons for
its maintenance. The custom, insofar as it is observed at all, is obviously connected with vote-getting: both Catholics and Jews constitute large and presumably somewhat solid voting blocs, and propitia-
tion is necessary to retain the favor of the gods of the voting booth.
For the same reason there has been some talk in recent years of
appointing a Negro. Sectional influences, already referred to, are of
some importance in this connection too; yet in recent times the
South has been heavily overrepresented on the Court, no doubt as a
result of the heavily Democratic orientation of Southerners. The
School Segregation decision of 1954—unanimous though it was—was
handed down by a Court containing three Southerners: Hugo Black
of Alabama, Stanley Reed of Kentucky, and Tom Clark of Texas; and
only a year earlier, before the death of Chief Justice Fred M. Vinson
of Kentucky, there had been four.

At times specific opinions have played a role in appointment. The
appointments of Justices William Strong and Joseph P. Bradley by
President Grant, with the apparent knowledge that they had expressed
opposition to the first Legal Tender decision, have already been mentioned. Theodore Roosevelt is said to have had one eye on the antitrust cases coming up when he appointed Holmes, but if he did he
was rather disappointed. And President Eisenhower probably appointed Justice William J. Brennan in 1956 at least partly to aid his
campaign for re-election, since Brennan was a Catholic Democrat from
a doubtful state.

In at least one recent instance personal friendship has accounted
in part for the presence of individuals on the Court. Justice Harold
Burton's selection was apparently due to no better reason than that
he was one of President Truman's "poker-playing pals" from Senate
days. It is also true, however, that there were no Republicans on the
Court at the time, a factor which may have had some influence on
the President's choice.

Possibly of greater importance than the other factors discussed is the necessity for senatorial approval of appointments. This has brought about a great and sometimes almost insurmountable pressure on a President to appoint men who are sponsored by (or at least acceptable to) influential senators, especially those who are members of the Committee on the Judiciary. The rise in 1954 of Senator James O. Eastland of Mississippi, a confirmed segregationist, to the chairmanship of this committee was consequently decried by some liberals who feared his power might be used to influence the type of judges appointed to the federal bench. While it is true that a determined effort by a popular President may force senatorial acceptance of an unwanted appointment—as in the case of Wilson's selection of Louis D. Brandeis—most have felt unable or unwilling to go to such lengths, and have been rather careful to sound out senatorial opinion thoroughly in advance of nomination. The deliberate actions of President Rutherford B. Hayes in the appointment of Justice John Marshall Harlan in 1877 may serve as an illustration, both of the influence of the Senate and of other aspects herein discussed.

After Justice David Davis resigned March 4, 1877, in order to become the senator from Illinois, President Hayes took under lengthy advisement the problem of filling the vacancy. In fact, his deliberations took eight months. During this time some two dozen men received at least limited consideration for the post. The following items were pre-eminent in Hayes's mind: he needed a Republican, for the Senate was controlled by the radicals and would brook no Democratic appointment; he wanted a Southerner, since there was none on the Court; and he wanted a moderate rather than a radical. The conflict between the radicals and the moderates—largely a fight between the executive and Congress—became the key to the appointment. Hayes found he would have to compromise on at least one of his requirements—for a Southerner would inevitably be a Democrat. At length it became apparent that there were two who were logical candidates for the post: Benjamin Bristow of Kentucky, and his law partner, John Harlan. Both were prominent Republican politicians and as close to being "real" Southerners as could be found in the party ranks. Bristow probably had the wider support, but he was suspected of having succumbed to "White House fever," and Hayes was warned by Justice Samuel F. Miller and others that the Court had been degraded sufficiently by the similar ambitions of Chief Justice Salmon P. Chase and of Justice Davis. Harlan had several points in his favor: he had fought for the Union both politically and militarily; he had secured Hayes's nomination at the 1876 convention by swinging the Kentucky delegation behind him; he had served on the controversial Hayes-appointed Louisiana electoral commission in the summer of 1877; and he could secure the support of many Democrats.

Under the circumstances of the fight over the executive prerogatives which Hayes was trying to recover from the radical Congress, anyone who had been appointed would have had serious difficulty in securing approval from the Senate. After carefully calculating the possibilities, Hayes sent Harlan's nomination forward on October 16, 1877. The fight over the appointment raged for forty-one days in the Judiciary Committee, with Senator Roscoe Conkling of New York, a leading radical, the primary figure in the opposition. While some attempt was made to impugn Harlan himself, the major aspect was opposition to Hayes. For a time it looked as though the nomination would be disapproved, but it finally secured the favorable report of the committee on November 26 and passed through the full Senate without further difficulty. Hayes had guessed correctly that with Democratic support Harlan's nomination would be approved. The approval may be regarded not only as a victory for Harlan, but as a gain for Hayes and the moderates. It might even be said to be one of the first steps in the end of reconstruction, which was the main point of contention between these two wings of the Republican party.

Thus the role of politics and the crucial part played by the Senate in Supreme Court appointments is clear. The Senate is an even more powerful influence in the case of appointments to the lower federal courts. This is due to the fact that, particularly in regard to the district courts, local influences are so much more powerful, as well as to the workings of that most weird of American political customs, senatorial courtesy. According to the rules of this game, the President is permitted to appoint men to political office within a state only after gaining the "advice and consent" of the senior senator of the President's party from that state—*not* of the Senate as a whole. President Franklin D. Roosevelt's famous quarrel with Senator Carter Glass of Virginia came as a result of Roosevelt's deliberate temerity in nominating for district judge one of that senator's political opponents. Other Presidents have encountered the same kind of hostile reaction, and they invariably lose such battles. Somewhat more leeway exists for the President in the not infrequent cases in which his party has no senator from the state where the vacancy is located, but even here party factors usually predominate. In 1961, Senator Russell Long's opposition to District Judge Skelly Wright's promotion to the Circuit Court of Appeals apparently prevented Judge Wright from being nominated for the post; Wright had made several decisions fostering integration in New Orleans schools. Later President John F. Kennedy solved this dilemma by nominating Judge Wright to a circuit judgeship in a different part of the country.

This analysis of the factors that operate in the appointment of judges has not been an exhaustive one. It has, for instance, paid no heed to the prior judicial experience of the candidate. The omission has been deliberate, for on the whole this has not been a significant factor. There have, of course, been occasions when lower court or state judges have been promoted to the Supreme Court; but lying behind their promotion will usually be found some other factor: party service, political opinions, or perhaps merely the feeling that public opinion would favor the appointment. This has been made clear in the quotation, given above, of Teddy Roosevelt regarding the appointment of Judge Oliver Wendell Holmes of the Massachusetts Supreme Court. Many factors, as we have seen, enter into an appointment, and of these factors judicial experience seems to be of minor importance.

The Qualifications of Judges

If prior judicial experience is not a prerequisite or even a very commonly held characteristic of the men appointed to the federal bench, what kinds of backgrounds are most important? Party, religion, and section are factors. But beyond these, what kind of man is most likely to become a judge? Only two significant generalizations apply: first, the appointee will be a lawyer; and second, he will almost always have been active in politics.

This does not mean that he will necessarily be actively engaged in the practice of law; he may, on the contrary, never have practiced. But he will have been through law school and will have passed his bar exams. *Usually* he will have practiced law at least as a side line, but his practicing days are likely to be far behind him at the time of his appointment.

Since the theme of this text is that most of the work of the courts is of a political rather than a strictly legal nature (and that this is especially true of the Supreme Court), it may be asked why it is necessary that only lawyers sit on the bench. The Soviet Union, for instance, uses "lay" judges. This is partly just a matter of custom; but more important, judges must deal with lawyers, they must handle legal cases, and even political questions must be dealt with in a legal framework. The background of the law is a valuable and, indeed, a necessary part of the judge's equipment, and even more so in the trial courts as compared with the appellate level.

The second generalization—that the appointee will have been actively engaged in politics—is not as invariable a rule as the first, as the case of Justice Holmes strikingly illustrates; but it is nevertheless the *general* rule. It does not mean that the candidate is holding any political office, though men have often proceeded to the bench from the Senate or from other high political or administrative posts. It may mean merely informal, behind-the-scenes political activity of the type exemplified by the career of Felix Frankfurter, who had never held any official position prior to donning the robe of a Supreme Court justice.

The Role of Individuals on the Supreme Court

The significance of the individual in the work of the Supreme Court has been a question of some debate. A few commentators (like Fred Rodell [35]) go so far as to say that the Court can only be realistically considered as a collection of nine men, who happen by coincidence to be sitting behind the same bar. To such writers every court decision cannot be understood except in terms of the individuals on the bench. It seems certain, however, that this view is extreme and therefore false.

At the same time it seems no more true to *ignore* the fact that the Court is made up of nine individuals. Some other writers have acted as if there were no such thing as dissent and disagreement among the nine, and as though even the 5 to 4 decisions of the Court could be regarded as entirely institutional products.

As so often is true, the middle ground between these extremes seems the most accurate. The Court is both a collection of nine men *and* an institution. It is a collection in the sense that it could not operate without its members, and consequently to understand its decisions the student needs a thorough knowledge of the men who are on the bench. On the other hand, the Court has a history and a tradition which surely could not be encompassed by a separate consideration of the lives of the several hundred men who have been justices since 1789. Though keeping in mind the institutional aspect of the Supreme Court, it is also essential to analyze the very real roles played by individuals.

At its extreme, the importance of an individual to the work of the Court cannot be better illustrated than by reference to the career of the man who by common consent is regarded as the greatest justice ever to sit on the Supreme Court bench: John Marshall. Marshall, who occupied the chair of the Chief Justice from 1801 to 1835, was chiefly instrumental in shaping judicial review and many of the basic principles of constitutional law as we know it today. His influence lay in two major personality characteristics: a subtle and dialectical mind, and a force of character so great that he completely dominated his colleagues on the bench. The result was that his personal ideas of constitutional interpretation became the ideas of the Court to an extent equaled by no subsequent judge. His influence was heightened by the fact that his tenure came during the formative period of the American Union, when the role that the courts were to play was still plastic enough to be molded to his desires. He wrote most of the opinions of the Court during his long tenure, and dissenting opinions were astonishingly rare, especially when compared to the record of the last twenty years. He wrote, from 1805 to 1833 (not his entire

[35] Fred Rodell, *Nine Men: A Political History of the Supreme Court of the United States* (New York: Random House, 1955), especially pp. 27–32.

term), 458 majority opinions out of a total of 977, dissenting himself
only half a dozen times. In addition, only 74 dissents were written by
others, many of these representing separate dissents in the same cases.
No justice has ever equaled this ascendancy or even approached it.
It remains a question how far Marshall was forced to accommodate
his opinions to those of his colleagues in order to maintain this unusual unanimity; the inner workings of the Court have never been
publicized. But it seems most likely that his persuasive gift was so
great that his judicial opinions as written represent largely his own
ideas rather than those of his associates.

Marshall represents the extreme. On the other side, there have been
periods when there was no single justice who stood out either in
influence or in ability over his brothers. Conspicuous in this regard was
the Court in the eleven years of its existence prior to Marshall's appointment, and probably also during the period (1864–73) of Salmon
P. Chase's chief justiceship. The men on the bench during these
times were of only average or mediocre ability or had been on the
bench for only a short time; none had the force of personality to
dominate his colleagues.

Most of the history of the Supreme Court lies between these two
extremes; the Marshall Court as well as those of the 1790's and the
1860's may be regarded as atypical. The more typical situation is a
Court with several members of above average ability and influence,
which is often exerted in opposing directions. Thus the Court in the
1920's contained such excellent men as Chief Justice Taft and Justice
Sutherland, who were conservatives, and Justices Holmes, Brandeis,
and Stone, who stood on the liberal side much of the time. Each of
these men was outstanding in his own right. In the 1930's an analogous
situation existed, with Chief Justice Charles Evans Hughes sitting together with the famous jurists Cardozo, Sutherland, Brandeis, and
Stone. The Court of the 1940's numbered, in addition to Chief
Justice Stone, at least two and possibly three men of above average
caliber in Felix Frankfurter, Hugo Black, and Robert H. Jackson.

It would be a mistake to assume that the role of individuals on the
Court is confined to the ability positively to lead the rest of the Court
as John Marshall did. Of almost equal importance is the man who,
through his criticism in conference or in dissent, can gradually shape
the opinions of his colleagues, of the legal profession, or of the general
public. This is the role for which John Marshall Harlan, Oliver
Wendell Holmes, and Louis D. Brandeis are known. In each instance
their powerful arguments, over a period of years, were adopted by
the public and the legal profession, with the result that eventually
new appointees to the Court made their dissents into majority doctrine.

A final point worth some consideration is the fact that the Chief
Justice, as "first among equals," has by virtue of his position the
opportunity—if he is strong enough—to exercise a good deal of in-

fluence over the Court. He "chairs" the judicial conference, assigns the writing of most opinions, and to some extent controls the procedure in Court sessions. These functions, in the hands of a strong man like Hughes, may give him an initial power which his very strength of character accentuates. Even a "weak" Chief Justice like Melville Fuller or Fred Vinson gains a certain stature and influence just because he is the *Chief* Justice. Probably a greater proportion of our chief justices have gained fame than the occupants of any other Supreme Court seat: Marshall, Roger Brooke Taney, William Howard Taft, Charles Evans Hughes, and Harlan Fiske Stone certainly would classify as front-rank justices.

That there are definite limitations to the influence that any one man, even a Marshall, can wield should need no emphasis if the reader has absorbed what has been said earlier in this chapter, and if he realizes that no justice has any real weapon with which to coerce. Influence on the Court is based on personality, sagacity, and respect. The fact that the decisions of the Court are officially institutional insulates justices to some extent from public criticism as individuals, and leaves them largely free to act as their legal knowledge, their social views, and their consciences dictate; but this does not mean that the institutional pressures of the traditions of the Court, of the law, and of the American political system can be ignored.

Psychoanalyzing Judges

The recent stress on the influence of individuals on the Court has led to a great deal of study among students of constitutional law of the backgrounds and personalities of judges. Judicial biographies now extant which try to "psychoanalyze" a judge and explain why he judged as he did have reached the number of about a dozen, and more are on the way. A mass of periodical literature utilizes the same approach, particularly in connection with Court decisions in specific cases. There is no denying that a thorough knowledge of the social background, family life, and political influences to which a judge has been exposed can make Court decisions more understandable; the effects of the frontier on such a man as Stephen J. Field, or of the study of legal philosophy on Benjamin Cardozo, no doubt had a great deal to do with the opinions they expressed on the bench.

As do most methods of studying the Court, this examination of "what the justice had for breakfast," nevertheless, has its limitations. For if a Sutherland be found, whose conservatism is attributed to his background as a corporation lawyer, what then of a Brandeis—a crusading liberal who also spent his legal career largely in corporation law? The truth is, unfortunately, that we do not know enough about the human mind and personality to rely too much on this sort of approach. Valuable though it be, reservations and qualifications must always be kept in mind when one is using it. While the social and economic background account for much, and while the justice's age may be a factor to consider, nevertheless three distinct limiting factors suggest themselves.

First, the influence of the law, with its pervasive tradition and rigid forms, must certainly operate to limit the extent to which the personality of an individual judge can govern his approach to any specific case. It may be that the state of the law makes his particular preference an impossible alternative, or that legal technicalities stand in the way even of taking a case. Second, the political ambitions of a judge, should he have any, may incline him to subordinate or accentuate his personal feelings about a case. If, as is not unknown, a judge harbors the hope that he may some day be President, his judicial opinions may be tailored to his ambition rather than to his philosophy. Third, one must consider the imponderability of the human equation. With all the advances made in modern psychology we still cannot be sure we know why human beings act the way they sometimes do, and the difficulties are multiplied when we consider that we cannot probe Supreme Court justices on a psychoanalyst's couch.

What Makes a Great Judge Great?

It would seem impossible to list positively the factors that may produce a great judge, and it is no more possible to predict in advance (with any reliability) who will be a great judge. Certainly there was little in John Marshall's political career or background to suggest that he would become our greatest justice. The same could be said of Harlan, of Stone, and of many other successful judges. One difficulty is that it depends not only on the man himself, but on the conditions existing while he is on the bench. Had Marshall sat one hundred years later than he did, his place in Court history would without doubt have been much different than it is, for to him was given the opportunity to shape the course of American constitutional history; yet his predecessors had much the same opportunity but failed to use it. The man needs the opportunity, but the opportunity does not necessarily produce the man.

The judgment of history, it must be added, is to a large extent a relative and changing judgment. A man who is considered great by this generation may recede into comparative insignificance in the assessment of the next, and conversely the man who stands for principles unappreciated during his life may emerge as a great man to another generation which accepts his values. Consequently even after a judge has retired or died it is not easy to draw up a definitive evaluation of his services on the bench.

Adding to the difficulty is the comparative lack of any accepted standard by which to measure the quality of a judge. Is he to be measured on his ability to divine and represent the dominant opinions of his own day? If so, not Marshall, but Field and perhaps even men like Edward D. White and Rufus Peckham would be considered great. Is the verdict rather to rest on how well he predicts the opinions of some future generation? Then Marshall, Harlan, and Holmes become great. Is our opinion dependent on the ability of the man as a jurist—a man of great legal skill and learning? The great judge then will not be Marshall; but Joseph Story, Horace Gray, Holmes, Cardozo, and Frankfurter will rank high. Or finally, is our judgment to rest on "the logic of the heart"—the man who represents the highest in human aspirations and who can write with a pen of fire: the crusader? Then we come back to Marshall, to Harlan, to Brandeis, and to Black.

No doubt, in the final analysis, a judgment of some kind is made by combining these varied standards of value. It is probable today that most constitutional scholars would rank Marshall, Taney, Holmes, Brandeis, Hughes, and Cardozo as our greatest Supreme Court justices. The disparity in types is so great as to cause one to wonder if the same standard of greatness is being applied for each! Some would add to this list—Story, Field, Harlan, Taft, Stone, and perhaps Miller. But whatever the list any individual may prefer, it remains true that the standards for judgment are inexact, vague, and fluctuating. As a result it is impossible to predict whether either Frankfurter or Black, or Chief Justice Warren, or the next appointee will be considered a great justice.

The Jurist's Art

This and the preceding chapter have attempted to bring together and analyze the multifarious factors that influence the American court system as it plays its part in the total political system of our nation. Walton Hamilton has, in a typically pungent statement, thus summarized:

> The art of judgment is of its own kind. Unlike the poet, the historian, or the essayist, the jurist cannot listen to the promptings of his own heart, choose the subject upon which he would write, say as he would all that is in his mind, and follow his interest to a fresh theme. Instead, as a member of a court his decisions are a mere step in the process of disposing of litigation. He cannot speak until the appropriate cause comes along, he can address himself to the larger issue only so far as a suit at law allows, he must express a partial opinion and wait for a suitable occasion to continue. Even when his concern is with constitutional issues, and in granting or withholding approval to statutes he is declaring public policy, his manner of speech cannot be that of the statesman. His place is in the institution of the judiciary; he is bound by its usages and procedures; he addresses himself, not directly to a social question, but to a matter of policy translated into the language of law; he cannot escape the values, rules, and intellectual ways of the discipline he professes.

On the frontier where a changing social necessity impinges upon the established law, the jurist must possess a double competence; he must employ alike
legal rule and social fact, and where they clash, as inevitably they will in a
developing culture, he must effect the best reconciliation that may lie between
them. The judge must become the statesman without ceasing to be the jurist;
the quality of his art lies in the skill, the intelligence, and the sincerity with
which he manages to serve two masters.[36]

Suggestions for Further Readings

The Limitations on Judicial Review

Most of the writings cited for Chapter VIII are relevant here. See
also Benjamin Cardozo, *The Nature of the Judicial Process* (New
Haven: Yale University Press, 1921) and the following articles:

Chase, Harold W. "The Warren Court and Congress," 44 *Minnesota
   Law Rev.* 595 (1960).
Elliott, Shelden D. "Court-Curbing Proposals in Congress," 33 *Notre
   Dame Lawyer* 597 (1958).
Pollitt, Daniel H. "Should the Court be 'Curbed,'" 37 *North
   Carolina Law Rev.* 17 (1958).
Ratner, Leonard G. "Congressional Power over the Appellate Juris-
   diction of the Supreme Court," 109 *Univ. of Pennsylvania Law
   Rev.* 157 (1960).

Grounds for Judicial Decision

The references for this section are found in the notes for Chapter
III.

The Selection and Influence of Judges

Few works have been written specifically on this topic. Reference
may be made to relevant sections of Glendon Schubert, *Quantitative
Analysis of Judicial Behavior* (Glencoe, Ill.: The Free Press, 1960);
John R. Schmidhauser, *The Supreme Court: Its Politics, Personalities,
and Procedures* (New York: Holt, Rinehart & Winston, 1960); and
Cortez E. M. Ewing, *Judges of the Supreme Court, 1789–1937*
(Minneapolis: University of Minnesota Press, 1938). The following
articles are also useful:

Beth, Loren P. "Judge into Justice: Should Supreme Court Appointees
   Have Judicial Experience?" 58 *South Atlantic Qtrly.* 521 (1959).
Frank, John P. "The Appointment of Supreme Court Justices: Prestige, Principles and Politics," 1941 *Wisconsin Law Rev.* 172, 343,
   461.

---

[36] Walton H. Hamilton, "The Jurist's Art," 31 *Columbia Law Rev.* 1073
(1931).

————. "Fred Vinson and the Chief Justiceship," 21 *Univ. of Chicago Law Rev.* 212 (1954).

Frankfurter, Felix. "The Supreme Court in the Mirror of Justices," 105 *Univ. of Pennsylvania Law Rev.* 791 (1957).

Kort, Fred. "Predicting Supreme Court Decisions Mathematically," 51 *Amer. Pol. Sci. Rev.* 1 (1957).

McKay, Robert B. "Selection of Supreme Court Justices," 9 *Kansas Law Rev.* 109 (1960).

Schmidhauser, John R. "The Justices of the Supreme Court—A Collective Portrait," 3 *Midwest Jnl. of Pol. Sci.* 1 (1959).

On the appointment of Mr. Justice Harlan, see Document: "The Appointment of Mr. Justice Harlan," 29 *Indiana Law Rev.* 46 (1953).

The writings on individual justices have now become so numerous as to defy listing. Only the more significant books are listed here:

Bent, Silas. *Justice Oliver Wendell Holmes* (New York: Garden City Pub. Co., 1932).

Beveridge, Arthur J. *The Life of John Marshall* (Boston: Houghton Mifflin Co., 1919).

Biddle, Francis. *Mr. Justice Holmes* (New York: Charles Scribner's Sons, 1942).

Bowen, Catherine D. *Yankee from Olympus* [Holmes] (Boston: Little, Brown & Co., 1944).

————. *The Lion and the Throne* [Lord Coke] (Boston: Little, Brown & Co., 1957).

Dunham, Alison, and Kurland, Philip B. *Mr. Justice* [a collection of essays] (Chicago: University of Chicago Press, 1956).

Fairman, Charles. *Mr. Justice Miller and the Supreme Court* (Cambridge: Harvard University Press, 1939).

Frank, John P. *Mr. Justice Black* (New York: Alfred A. Knopf, 1948).

Frankfurter, Felix. *Mr. Justice Holmes and the Supreme Court* (Cambridge: Harvard University Press, 1938).

Hellman, George S. *Benjamin N. Cardozo—American Judge* (New York: McGraw-Hill Book Co., 1940).

Hendel, Samuel. *Charles Evans Hughes and the Supreme Court* (New York: King's Crown Press, 1951).

Howe, Mark deWolfe. *Justice Oliver Wendell Holmes* [a multivolumed work some of which is not yet published] (Cambridge: Harvard University Press, 1957–   ).

King, Willard L. *Melville Weston Fuller* (New York: The Macmillan Co., 1950).

Konefsky, Samuel. *Chief Justice Stone and the Supreme Court* (New York: The Macmillan Co., 1946).

————. *The Legacy of Holmes and Brandeis* (New York: The Macmillan Co., 1956).

Lief, Alfred. *Brandeis: The Personal History of an American Ideal* (New York: Stackpole Sons, 1936).

Loth, David. *Chief Justice: John Marshall and the Growth of the Republic* (New York: W. W Norton, 1949).

McLean, Joseph E. *William Rufus Day* (Baltimore: Johns Hopkins Press, 1946).

Mason, Alpheus T. *Brandeis: A Free Man's Life* (New York: The Viking Press, 1946).

————. *Harlan Fiske Stone, Pillar of the Law* (New York: The Viking Press, 1956).

Morgan, Donald G. *Justice William Johnson: The First Dissenter* (Columbia: University of South Carolina Press, 1954).

Palmer, Benjamin W. *Marshall and Taney: Statesmen of the Law* (Minneapolis: University of Minnesota Press, 1939).

Paschal, Joel F. *Mr. Justice Sutherland: A Man against the State* (Princeton: Princeton University Press, 1951).

Pollard, J. P. *Mr. Justice Cardozo: A Liberal Mind in Action* (New York: Yorktown Press, 1935).

Pringle, Henry. *The Life and Times of William Howard Taft* (New York: Farrar & Rinehart, 1939).

Pusey, Merlo J. *Charles Evans Hughes* (New York: The Macmillan Co., 1951).

Swisher, Carl B. *Stephen J. Field, Craftsman of the Law* (Washington: Brookings Institution, 1930).

————. *Roger B. Taney* (New York: The Macmillan Co., 1935).

Thomas, Helen S. *Felix Frankfurter: Scholar on the Bench* (Baltimore: Johns Hopkins Press, 1960).

Williams, Charlotte. *Hugo L. Black: A Study in the Judicial Process* (Baltimore: Johns Hopkins Press, 1950).

The periodical literature on individual judges is so immense that no purpose would be served by attempting to list it here. Students can trace much of it for the judge of their choice by culling the *Index to Legal Periodicals* and the two general indexes, *Reader's Guide* and *Public Affairs Information Service*.

CHAPTER VI

The Courts as
Political Agents:
The 1937 Revolution

Today it may be the Court which is charged with forgetting its constitutional duties. Tomorrow it may be the Congress. The next day it may be the executive. If we yield to temptation now to lay the lash upon the Court we are only teaching others how to apply it to ourselves and to the people when the occasion seems to warrant.

—SENATE JUDICIARY COMMITTEE REPORT, 1937

In March of 1933 President Franklin D. Roosevelt took office in the midst of the greatest domestic crisis the United States has ever experienced except for the Civil War. Business was practically at a standstill; 12,000,000 workers were unemployed; the bread line had become a common urban sight; banks were failing by the hundreds; farmers by the thousands were being forced off their farms by foreclosures. It seemed, indeed, that the American economy was on the verge of complete collapse. It also seemed to many Americans that the political system was unable to cope with the disaster; at the least, it was thought that some drastic changes in our polity would be necessary. Could the national government, operating under the terms of a charter 144 years old, find in that charter the powers to deal with an emergency on such a grand scale? Actions unprecedented would be necessary—did the Constitution permit such actions? And what would be the effects of judicial review on such actions as Congress and the President might take? Would the judges see and use the elastic generalities of the aged document so as to permit drastically new

111

governmental programs? Or would they insist upon a strict and traditional reading? Upon the answer might depend in large measure not
only the ability of the government to meet the existing crisis, but
also its capacity to forestall future calamities of similar nature. It is
not too much to say that upon the answer might also depend the
life of the Constitution itself.

Roosevelt's New Deal and the reaction of the Supreme Court to
it, therefore, provide the best possible illustration of the conclusions
of the preceding chapters. If the courts are in truth political agents,
the fact should show up most clearly in periods when new and unprecedented policy is being made. In addition, the effects of the New
Deal on the Supreme Court were so great as, in the opinion of some
experts, to affect its powers and prestige far into the future.

The Political, Social, and Legal Background

The events of the 1930's, at least so far as they involved the
Supreme Court, had been a long time a-building. Back in the 1880's
the Court had allied itself with American corporate enterprise by
acquiescing in the construction of the substantive due process doctrines
which had as their aim the protection of corporate business from
interference by state legislatures. With the state's use of the police
power thus partially blocked, the federal government entered the
regulatory picture; but the Supreme Court, "upholding the federal
balance," emasculated the antitrust laws, curtailed for some time the
powers of the regulatory commissions, and prevented effective federal
action against child labor. Thus by judicial interpretation was con-
structed a "twilight zone" in which neither the police powers of the
states nor the delegated powers of the federal government could be
constitutionally exercised.

Even as early as 1895 there were objections to this Court policy,
both by laymen and lawyers—and also, significantly, by judges themselves. The dissents of John M. Harlan in the antitrust cases and of
Oliver Wendell Holmes and Louis D. Brandeis in the substantive due
process cases had come to be widely accepted in the country at large
long before the 1930's.

The problem was obscured, however, as long as the nation remained predominantly prosperous, for the demand for social and economic legislation during good times was never persistent enough to
force its acceptance over legal obstacles. As a result, when Roosevelt
entered the White House matters stood essentially as they had forty
or fifty years earlier. Roosevelt came into office pledged to "do something" about the calamitous state of affairs. It is true that he apparently did not quite know what he would do, and it is true that
the early New Deal legislation was consequently hastily and hap-
hazardly conceived and executed. But it is also true that New Deal

legislation built in substance on proposals that had been made many times in the years before 1933, and that these proposals were, in the minds of many constitutional scholars, within the constitutional means of Congress. There was thus nothing particularly shocking about most New Deal laws, though many of them undoubtedly seemed radical to the business community.

The Supreme Court, in spite of its past record, was somewhat of an unknown quantity because of the presence on the bench of several known liberals. The issue was therefore in doubt, and the personalities and tendencies of the individual judges were closely scanned by the politically weather-wise. On the conservative side were the famous "Four Horsemen of Conservatism"—Butler, McReynolds, Sutherland, and Van Devanter.

Pierce Butler was born and grew up in Minnesota during its frontier period. When Roosevelt took office Butler was sixty-seven years old. He was a Republican who had been appointed to the Court by President Harding. Fearless and industrious, forceful and argumentative, Butler was a sort of storm center in judicial conference, for he was always willing to uphold his side of an argument and was not always careful to restrain his Irish temper, especially where Justice Brandeis was concerned. More important, Butler was an extreme conservative of the laissez-faire variety, who believed that the Constitution contained broad and specific guaranties of property rights.

James C. McReynolds, then seventy-one years old, was a Southern Democrat who had been appointed by President Wilson after a varied career including a law professorship at Vanderbilt, legal practice in New York, and various governmental posts culminating in the attorney generalship. Chief Justice Taft had called him "a continual grouch"; he was an acid and cantankerous bachelor who, in addition to opposing Brandeis' liberalism, was also violently anti-Semitic—so much so that the court dinners held by Chief Justice Hughes had to be split so that he and Brandeis would not be brought together socially. Like Butler, McReynolds had narrow and inflexible constitutional views.

George Sutherland, a learned and conscientious jurist, was also seventy-one. He had a very broad political background. Brought up in Utah, he served in the state legislature and in both houses of Congress, where he made a wide reputation as a senator. He had been an active Taft supporter in the campaign of 1912 when the Republican split occurred, had supported Harding, and had served as president of the American Bar Association before being appointed to the Supreme Court by Harding in 1922. He was a gentle and kindly man but nevertheless had something of a reputation as a raconteur. One biographer gives this instance: Justice Holmes, who loved a good story, would often enter the judicial conference, make straight for Sutherland, "and bending over so low that their heads were almost touching, longingly plead: 'Sutherland, J., tell me a story!'" And apparently Sutherland always obliged.[1] Consequently, in spite of his differences with his liberal colleagues, Sutherland was well liked on the Court. His conservatism was more philosophical and flexible than that of Butler or McReynolds, but he was usually found on the same side when economic issues were presented to the Court.

The fourth conservative was Willis Van Devanter. He was seventy-four, and had been raised in Indiana, going to Wyoming when he was twenty-five. There he became known as a skilled lawyer, with much of his practice coming from lumber and cattle interests and the Union Pacific Railroad. He had served in the Wyoming legislature and as chief justice of the state's supreme court, had been appointed to the federal circuit court in 1903 by Theodore Roosevelt, and was promoted to the Supreme Court by Taft in 1910. He was a courteous and genial gentleman who got on well with his colleagues. He had great difficulty in putting his thoughts on paper and therefore was not assigned as many opinions to write as were most of his brethren.

The four noted above had in common a belief in negative government, especially where economic affairs were concerned. It is noteworthy, in considering why, that all four (in distinct contrast to the rest of the justices) had grown up in rural or even frontier conditions, a situation that gave rise to the following analysis (of Butler) by Attorney General Biddle:

> He was brought up in a school of thought which had not learned to doubt the implications of its perhaps over-simplified assumptions—laissez-faire, individualism, free competition. These things meant the American way. By this way he had come to the top and the failure of others to arrive seemed to indicate personal fault rather than economic disadvantage. The frontiers were open. Success was at the end of a straight road.[2]

It seems probable that the frontier conditions were more influential than the fact that each of the four was a "self-made" man, for most of the other justices—more liberal though they were—had also risen from circumstances that were not too favorable and had made reputations and some wealth for themselves. The frontier, and American agriculture as well, seemed to foster an individualism and self-reliance, and a feeling that a man became what he earned, that were not present in the eastern cities where the other five justices had earned their spurs. In this respect, then, it may be said that the "Four Horsemen" were representative of an older and declining aspect of American civilization. For America was no longer a nation of farmers and frontiersmen, but a nation of urban shopkeepers, factory workers, and industrialists. As much as anything else, it was probably the failure

---

[1] Joel F. Paschal, *Mr. Justice Sutherland: A Man against the State* (Princeton: Princeton University Press, 1951), p. 116.

[2] Memorial to Justice Butler, appearing in 310 U.S at p. vi (1939).

of the four to realize through experience the impact of this drastic change which accounted for their conservatism and their willingness—nay, eagerness—to embody it in the Constitution.

On the left side of the Court were three justices: Brandeis, Cardozo, and Stone. The aging Louis D. Brandeis, then seventy-seven, was the Jewish son of a Louisville merchant, who made a reputation and a fortune as a corporation lawyer in Boston before giving up his corporate practice and devoting his time to being "the people's advocate." Brandeis possessed a brilliant mind and a crusading temperament. His liberal tendencies had caused his nomination by Wilson to be strongly opposed in the Senate, and since his appointment he had not become less liberal, making a name for himself in dissent. He is also known for having developed, as mentioned before, the famous "Brandeis brief," in which all the ascertainable social and economic arguments were added to the legal ones in arguing before the courts.

Benjamin N. Cardozo, who was sixty-three, had gained a national reputation as a jurist while serving for years as Chief Judge of the New York Court of Appeals. A Hoover appointee, he nevertheless proved to be, not perhaps a liberal economically, but a "loose constructionist" on constitutional matters, which made him often *look* liberal. Cardozo, also Jewish, was a scholar of the law, somewhat of a recluse, a mild and gentle man who was respected and admired by everyone.

Justice Harlan Fiske Stone was a New York lawyer and former dean of the Columbia University Law School. A Republican aged sixty-one, he had been Coolidge's attorney general before his appointment by "Silent Cal" to the Supreme Court in 1925. Like Cardozo, his constitutional inclinations were toward a broad interpretation of federal power even though he was not necessarily an economic liberal. This slant did not please his Republican colleagues: Chief Justice Taft had said of him, "a learned lawyer in many ways, but his judgments I do not consider altogether safe." Stone was a big hearty man who liked people and got along well with most; his unwillingness to cut off argument was a handicap to the work of the Court when he later became Chief Justice.

The three "liberals" had in common only two things: all had maintained their careers in large cities, and all were scholars of the law rather than merely legal practitioners. They drew from their urban experiences a keen appreciation of the changes wrought in American society by the industrial revolution, and a feeling that democratic legislatures could ordinarily be trusted—at least in the economic field—and thus should not be interfered with by courts in their attempts to solve pressing economic and social problems.

The other two members of the Court—Hughes and Roberts—were the "swing men." They constituted the balance of power; if either of them voted with the "Four Horsemen," conservatism carried the day;

if neither did, liberalism was the victor. They were consequently the most important members of the Court, and the ones to whom lawyers' arguments would primarily be directed.

Charles Evans Hughes was probably the leading Republican politician of his day. At seventy-one, he could look back on a long and varied career which had brought him practically every political honor possible to an American, except the Presidency itself—an office that he lost only by the margin of California's electoral votes. He had been Governor of New York, Associate Justice of the United States Supreme Court, the Republican presidential nominee in 1916, Secretary of State, president of the American Bar Association, and a highly successful practicing attorney. Hughes was something of a liberal; his tendencies were to vote with the Brandeis wing of the Court, but this was sufficiently doubtful that it could not be counted on. Some of his critics, in fact, have accused him of trimming his sails to the prevailing winds.

Owen J. Roberts was the ninth member. A comparative youngster of fifty-eight, he had been an extremely successful lawyer in Philadelphia, a law professor at the University of Pennsylvania, and Assistant District Attorney of Philadelphia. He was appointed to the Court in 1930 by President Hoover. He was either a mild liberal or a mild conservative, depending on the outlook of the observer, but seems essentially to have had no very pronounced convictions as to the function of the courts. He was the most unpredictable, and thus the most important, justice on this divided court.

As will be noted later, the line-ups given above were not invariable, especially on the liberal side. Nevertheless the major question in the majority of the New Deal cases was, "How will Hughes and Roberts vote?"

In cases from the states under the police power, the Court took a varying line during the depression years, but primarily continued the old policy of strict limitations of state power. Thus, in the *New State Ice Co. Case,* state regulation of the ice industry was voided despite a vigorous dissent by Brandeis;[3] in *Colgate* v. *Harvey* a state income tax discriminating against income from loans outside the state was vetoed;[4] and in the *Tipaldo Case* a minimum wage law for women was rejected.[5] On the other hand, a Minnesota mortgage moratorium law[6] was upheld, as was a New York milk price-fixing law.[7]

But the crux of the issue was the federal power. Never before had the national government attempted to control prices, to enforce collective bargaining, to impose agricultural controls, or to devalue the

[3] *New State Ice Co.* v. *Liebmann,* 285 U.S. 262 (1932).
[4] *Colgate* v. *Harvey,* 296 U.S. 404 (1935).
[5] *Morehead* v. *New York* ex rel. *Tipaldo,* 298 U.S. 587 (1936).
[6] *Home Building & Loan Association* v. *Blaisdell,* 290 U.S. 398 (1934).
[7] *Nebbia* v. *New York,* 291 U.S. 502 (1934).

currency. The Court's treatment of these issues was vastly more significant than its handling of the state cases.

Roosevelt and his "Brain Trust," being politicians faced with an important and immediate problem, did not look at social and economic questions from primarily a constitutional point of view, but rather from a practical one. Nevertheless there was contained in most of the New Deal legislation a respectable constitutional theory dating back at least as far as Lincoln and probably as far as Hamilton. In one aspect this was the idea that emergencies furnish the occasion for the exercise of powers not normally used by government; but more commonly the broad interpretation of the necessary and proper clause and the implied powers was relied upon to give the commerce, taxing, and spending powers a new reach and scope. The justification for the Agricultural Adjustment Act or the National Industrial Recovery Act was essentially the same as the argument used by Hamilton for the Bank of the United States: that the Constitution should be read broadly, with its entire objectives in mind, rather than in a narrow manner using each clause as an isolated point.

There can be no doubt that both sides in the New Deal controversies were subconsciously reading their own economic and social philosophies into the Constitution. The New Dealers found by some alchemy that the very things they felt had to be done were permitted by the Constitution. For their part, the conservatives tended to regard the Constitution as Holy Writ enforcing the principles of laissez-faire individualism. If a constitution is to endure, the long-run view must be closer to that of the New Dealers, for in no other way can a charter written in one social milieu be adapted to another. So the New Deal had the force of history on its side even if the strictly constitutional arguments were about even. The Hamiltonian theory of constitutional construction has always in the long pull won out over the Jeffersonian because it makes better sense in an evolving world such as the one we live in. Nevertheless, for a time it seemed as if the majority of the Supreme Court was willing to destroy the Court and the Constitution in a futile attempt to hold back the march of time.

The New Deal Cases: Pre-1937

The first important case to arise after the New Dealers took office —and a storm signal for the future—was the *Hot Oil Case*. In an attempt to cope with overproduction, low prices, and wasteful competition in the oil industry, the government had set up a code of fair practices for the industry. One of the provisions authorized the President, in his discretion, to prohibit the shipment in interstate commerce of any oil produced in violation of the state quota laws. The Court did not deal with the validity of the code itself, but with the Presi·

dent's power under the law to prohibit interstate shipment. On January 7, 1935, Chief Justice Hughes spoke for an eight-man majority in holding, for the first time in American history, that a law was void because of the delegation by Congress of too much legislative power to the President. Only Justice Cardozo dissented; he felt that the delegation was both legitimate in the circumstances and within constitutional limits.[8]

The government won a narrow and somewhat inconclusive victory in the *Gold Clause Cases*. Faced with a monetary and financial collapse, it had used the constitutional power to "coin Money" and "regulate the Value thereof" to devalue the dollar by decreasing its gold content. The result was that private contracts with clauses requiring payment in gold at the standard used when the contract was made were called into question, as were government contracts stipulating value in the old currency. The American dollar had never before been treated so unceremoniously; there was understandably a great outcry from "sound money" people and creditors.

By the time the *Gold Clause Cases* reached the Supreme Court the law had been in effect for eighteen months; its nullification would have resulted in financial chaos. The decision came down February 18, 1935. Chief Justice Hughes, again speaking for the majority in two 5 to 4 decisions, refused to invalidate the law.[9] As to the private contracts, he held that no private contracts could diminish the legitimate powers of Congress, so that gold clauses in private contracts could be nullified by Congress in the exercise of the money power. As to government obligations, the Chief Justice read the government a long lecture on the unethical nature of its act, which amounted (he said) to the repudiation of its pledged word. It is rather obvious that he regarded the act as unconstitutional in this aspect; but instead of saying so, he went on to point out that the creditor had not lost money in real purchasing power as a result of the act and would, in fact, be unjustly enriched should he be paid in the old standard. Since he could prove no loss he had no legal case and no award could be given.

So the government won the practical victory, and like Marshall in the *Marbury Case*, Hughes was able to perform the masterly feat of castigating the government for acting unconstitutionally while yet refusing to use the Court's power to do anything about it! No case could so well illustrate the alternatives often available to judges, nor the superb political sense that the Court upon occasion can show. Pusey, in his biography of Hughes, says that seven judges thought the law unconstitutional as applied to government obligations: but only four felt called upon to dissent from the ruling, and they could afford to since

---

[8] *Panama Refining Co.* v. *Ryan*, 293 U.S. 388 (1935).
[9] *Norman* v. *Baltimore & Ohio R.R. Co.*, 294 U.S. 240 (1935); *Noritz* v. *United States*, 294 U.S. 317 (1935); and *Perry* v. *United States*, 294 U.S. 330 (1935).

they were not in the majority.[10] It is quite possible that their dissent was a luxury which some of them might not have indulged had their votes counted.

The victory for Roosevelt was uncomfortably narrow, even so, and gave no promise that other New Deal legislation would be treated so tenderly. May 6, 1935, saw the invalidation of the Railroad Retirement Act of 1934. This act had provided for a compulsory retirement and pension system for railway employees. Justice Roberts and the Four Horsemen said that Congress had no power to pass such a law in any form under the Commerce Clause. Hughes led the other four in a stinging dissent, accusing the majority of using its economic preferences as a guide instead of the Constitution:

> The power committed to Congress to govern interstate commerce does not require that its government should be wise, much less that it should be perfect. The power implies a broad discretion and thus permits a wide range even of mistakes.[11]

Three weeks later the Court struck a triple blow at the New Deal before adjourning for the summer. It unanimously struck down the Frazier-Lemke Act, which attempted to relieve farmers in their mortgage problems.[12] Again unanimously, it refused to permit the President to fire a member of the Federal Trade Commission who had been blocking the administration's policies on the Commission.[13] But most important was the decision invalidating the National Industrial Recovery Act. This act had authorized the setting up of industry-wide codes of fair practice, in an attempt to eliminate extreme competition and stabilize prices during the depression emergency. By the time the act came before the Court it had become largely ineffective, but the Court's decision was nevertheless awaited with much interest, as there was the possibility that Congress might overhaul the law in order to make it more effective. However, in the so-called "sick chicken" case the Court maintained that the NIRA was an unconstitutional delegation of legislative power to the executive, and that it was also a violation of the Commerce Clause. Actually either ground would have been sufficient to kill the law.[14]

The National Industrial Recovery Act was probably the "magnificent failure" of the Roosevelt administration. It was the greatest departure from traditional ideas of proper legislation. Many observers felt that it was a failure regardless of what the Court might do with it, but this was not the point. The use of delegation of power was almost

[10] Merlo J. Pusey, *Charles Evans Hughes* (New York: The Macmillan Co., 1951), Vol. II, p. 737.

[11] *Railroad Retirement Board v. Alton R.R. Co.,* 295 U.S. 330 (1935).

[12] *Louisville Bank v. Radford,* 295 U.S. 555 (1935).

[13] *Humphrey's Executor v. United States,* 295 U.S. 602 (1935).

[14] *Schechter Poultry Corp. v. United States,* 295 U.S. 495 (1935).

completely new as a constitutional principle to invalidate legislation; and the Court had once more refused to use a realistic modern interpretation of what constitutes interstate commerce. But the decision was unanimous, and little is to be gained from quibbling over the nuances of the opinions. Even Cardozo wrote that "this is delegation running riot."

This shattering blow to New Deal hopes seemed to carry with it the certainty that much other Roosevelt legislation would be voided. It was perhaps this certainty as much as the decision itself that led President Roosevelt a few days later to accuse the Court of trying to return the country to a "horse and buggy" approach to interstate commerce. And in truth for some time it seemed to be so. New Deal statutes were guillotined with almost monotonous regularity. On January 6, 1936, the Court—this time split 6 to 3—held unconstitutional the Agricultural Adjustment Act of 1933. To cope with the low prices and surpluses with which farmers were plagued, the act provided for a processing tax on manufacturers who processed agricultural goods; this tax was passed on to the consumer in a higher price. After the act had been in effect for over two years, with some success, it reached the Supreme Court. The tax was ruled invalid because it was used for benefit payments; the benefit payments were unconstitutional because, said the Court, Congress could not spend money on farmers since farming was essentially a local occupation under the control of the states. Justice Stone dissented for the three liberals, calling the decision a "tortured construction of the Constitution," and chiding the judges for exceeding their powers in declaring invalid a law to which the only objection was that it was unwise. Once more, then, a judge was accusing his colleagues of legislating rather than adjudicating.[15]

Various laws—some of them not specifically part of the New Deal—were also upheld. The amendment of the Trading with the Enemy Act,[16] the National Bankruptcy Act,[17] the Silver Purchase Act,[18] the Ashurst-Sumners Act,[19] and the Chaco Arms Embargo Act[20] all successfully ran the judicial gauntlet. Of these, however, only two were of any importance in the economic program of the New Deal. The Court also upheld the power of the government to build and operate Wilson Dam on the Tennessee River.[21]

---

[15] *United States* v. *Butler*, 297 U.S. 1 (1936).
[16] *Woodson* v. *Deutsche Gold und Silber Scheideanstalt Vormals Roesslor*, 292 U.S. 449 (1934).
[17] *Continental Illinois National Bank & Trust Co.* v. *Chicago, Rock Island & Pacific Ry. Co.*, 294 U.S. 648 (1935).
[18] *United States* v. *Hudson*, 299 U.S. 498 (1937).
[19] *Kentucky Whip & Collar Co.* v. *Illinois Central R.R. Co.*, 299 U.S. 334 (1937).
[20] *United States* v. *Curtiss-Wright Export Corp.*, 299 U.S. 304 (1936).
[21] *Ashwander* v. *TVA*, 297 U.S. 288 (1936).

But then the Court limited by statutory construction the powers of the newly created Securities and Exchange Commission, with Justice Sutherland in reality excoriating the government for having created the commission at all.[22] In the spring of 1936 the Court went on to strike down the Municipal Bankruptcy Act of 1934, with Hughes and the liberals dissenting.[23] And finally the judges adjourned for the summer after invalidating the Guffey Coal Act, which had attempted to rescue the coal industry from depression by using the code idea, fixing prices, requiring collective bargaining, and also setting up some controls over wages and working conditions. In a 5 to 4 vote, with Hughes again siding with the minority, the Court majority spoke through Justice Sutherland to say that the whole act was unconstitutional as an excessive stretching of the commerce power. Hughes thought that the price-fixing was valid but the labor regulations were invalid. The three liberals regarded the entire act as constitutional.[24]

By the end of the Court term in June of 1936, then, the Supreme Court had struck down seven major New Deal statutes; two of them by 5 to 4 majorities and two by 6 to 3. The New Deal seemed in a fair way to be destroyed by judicial fiat.

Roosevelt's Court-Packing Plan, 1937

The following November the voters of the United States returned Franklin D. Roosevelt to office with a huge majority, and the largest Congressional party majority in American history. The voters and the Supreme Court were thus in rather obvious disagreement. Roosevelt, not unnaturally, regarded the result as a mandate for the continuation of the New Deal and also, perhaps, as a public rebuke to the Court. He felt that the conservatives on the Court had deliberately remained on the bench beyond a proper age in order to thwart the New Deal and in the hope of holding their seats for Republicans. By 1936 six justices were over seventy; none had signified an intention of retiring; and Roosevelt had not yet had the opportunity of appointing a single justice.

Consequently one of Roosevelt's first acts after the election was to set his Attorney General, Homer Cummings, the task of developing a plan for "reforming" the Supreme Court. The peculiar direction that the plan took was apparently the result of the President's conviction that there was nothing particularly wrong with the Court as an institution: it was the men on the Court who were at fault. This idea led naturally to the result that the major emphasis was on giving the

[22] *Jones v. Securities & Exchange Commission*, 298 U.S. 1 (1936).
[23] *Ashton v. Cameron County Water Improvement District*, 298 U.S. 513 (1936).
[24] *Carter v. Carter Coal Co.*, 298 U.S. 238 (1936).

President an opportunity to appoint some new men to the bench. Thus the necessity for any major constitutional change was averted, and the President doubtless felt that it would be easier to get a simple Congressional act than a constitutional amendment.

The plan as it was finally developed had one major provision so far as the Supreme Court was concerned, which had the objective of encouraging justices to retire at the age of seventy. This controversial section proposed that for each justice who failed to retire at seventy, one additional justice should be added to the Court up to a maximum of fifteen. Since six justices were at the moment over the retirement age, this would have meant that the President could immediately appoint six new justices, who with the three liberals already on the Court would give the New Deal the necessary votes to carry the day. The strategy of Mr. Roosevelt was a calculated one: he refused to attack the Court directly on the major grounds that it was "legislating" or substituting its judgment of the wisdom of legislation for that of Congress; he did not even attack it for being a nineteenth-century court. Instead he concentrated his fire on the question of the ability of the older members of the Court to keep up with their work. The powers of the Supreme Court, then, were to be left untouched even in debate. All that was involved was a little judicial face-lifting.

Most commentators agree that the indirection indulged in by the President, instead of aiding in the passage of the bill, worked against it. Even its supporters, like the liberal Senator George Norris, confessed that they would have preferred a frontal attack. In addition, the ground chosen by the President proved to be the very point at which the Court was least vulnerable. The charge that the Court was unable to do its work could be challenged by the Court itself—and was—without the need for the judges to jump openly into the political controversy, whereas a direct attack on the decisions that had been made would have forced the Court to remain silent on the side lines or become overtly political. And of course the concentration on age was likely to produce a reverse reaction on the part of the liberal members of the Court; Brandeis was the oldest member of the Court, and Hughes was also over seventy. Finally, Roosevelt's ruse was rather transparent; the nation knew what was being attempted and public discussion was pretty much focused on the real issues despite the President's attempt to avoid them.

Public reaction to the proposal was sharply antagonistic—a fact which it took Roosevelt himself a long time to realize. The press almost unanimously opposed the plan. After all, the size of the Court had remained at nine since reconstruction days: it was popularly regarded as being a part of the Constitution. Conservatives therefore accused Roosevelt of trying to make himself a dictator by gaining control of the courts, and of course he was also charged with trying to achieve by indirection something that could not have been done directly. Nevertheless, the President's political prestige was so great, and his party majority in Congress so large, that for some time it was assumed that his bill would pass with little difficulty. The bill was introduced in February, 1937; in late March it still looked as though it would pass in substantially its original form.

The Attitude of the Supreme Court

Although little is known positively of the reactions of the judges of the Supreme Court to Roosevelt's re-election or to his scheme to reorganize the judiciary, certain logical assumptions can be made. For one thing, the middle men on the Court—Hughes and Roberts, perhaps particularly the latter—were undoubtedly much impressed by the size of the majority given the President in November. To a judge who realizes how dependent the power and prestige of his Court is on its place in public affection, the re-election of Roosevelt could not help but provide food for reflection. If it were true that the Supreme Court follows the election returns, no election could have provided a more forceful lead than that of 1936.

At the same time there can be little doubt that the members of the Court were shocked and affronted—and perhaps a little frightened—by the nature of the plan proposed by the President. It is not, after all, unlikely that at least some of the conservatives actually were trying to outlast the President in order to hold their seats for other conservatives. Not only did it now look as though it might be impossible to outlive the New Deal regime, but it also appeared that the old fox in the White House was going to outflank them anyway. But even the liberals like Brandeis and Cardozo, men wholeheartedly committed to the Court as an institution, could not stomach the President's proposal.

It therefore seemed desirable for the Court to do what it could to prevent the passage of the court bill. Three courses of action presented themselves, and all, whether or not deliberately, were used. First, the Court could fight the President's plan by making it appear unnecessary on the grounds that Roosevelt had chosen—that the Court was behind in its work. This need not be openly political, for it could be presented as a mere matter of statistics. Senator Burton K. Wheeler of Montana, who informally headed the Senate opposition to the bill, had first asked Chief Justice Hughes to appear before the Judiciary Committee of the Senate. The Chief Justice, not loath to comply but feeling that it would be better if that impeccably liberal Democrat, Brandeis, went along, asked the aged justice to accompany him. But the venerable liberal strongly opposed such a move, feeling that it was too obviously political and would thus be improper. Then Hughes himself suggested that a letter be written to the committee. With this suggestion Brandeis concurred. In the Chief Justice's words:

Later—on Saturday, as I recall it—Senator Wheeler, who I understood had seen Brandeis in the interval, called on me and asked me to write such a letter. He said that the Committee desired this letter so that it could be used on Monday morning at the opening of the hearing on behalf of the opponents of the bill. This gave me very limited time but I proceeded at once to assemble the necessary data, and on Sunday, March 21st, the letter was completed. I at once took it to Justice Brandeis and to Justice Van Devanter, and each went over it carefully and approved it.[25]

The three justices—one liberal, one conservative, and one in the middle—thus rather openly joined the opposition to the bill. Their letter pointed out that the Supreme Court was not behind in its work (as indeed, under Hughes's firm generalship, it was not), and then went on to imply that the Court felt that an increase in the number of justices was a bad policy, and concluded by saying that such an increase would make the Court less efficient and less able to do its work.

This letter rather conclusively dispelled the notion that the judges of the Court were Olympian deities seated aloof from mundane politics in their marble palace. Its purpose was obvious, and nothing the justices could have done would have shown more clearly their opposition to the court bill.

A second way of taking the steam out of the bill was to allow Roosevelt to make some appointments to the Court. This would mean, of course, that someone must resign. In order to prove that no one was deliberately staying on the bench, the resigning justice had to be a conservative. In addition to indicating that conservatives were willing to allow Roosevelt an appointment, the resignation would also permit the administration to give up the bill with good grace, since its major objective—a change in the personnel of the court—would have been accomplished. So, on May 18, Justice Van Devanter announced his retirement as of the end of the term. Hughes denied any attempt to influence Van Devanter; apparently the major push came from Senator William E. Borah of Idaho. But there is no doubt that all the members of the Court appreciated the political effects which the resignation would have, for the fact that even this one resignation would alter the whole complexion of the Court was obvious. With Hughes voting quite often with the liberals, and with a new liberal on the bench, this would change the 5 to 4 votes to the liberal side.

The third course open to the Court was to revise its attitude toward New Deal legislation. The reversal, which came in the spring of 1937, was too startling to have been entirely accidental, even though Chief Justice Hughes (who should know) always maintained that the matter was never discussed by the Court or by him with any other justice. The justices were well aware that it was their decisions, not their ages, which constituted the real issue; and they could hardly have ignored

---

[25] Pusey, *op. cit.*, Vol. II, p. 755.

the fact that a change in the pattern of decision would most effectively cut the ground from under the packing bill. At the same time, it was no doubt useless to try to sway any of the four conservatives: regardless of necessity, they were determined to stick to their beliefs. That meant that any change in attitude had to come from the men in the middle —Hughes and Roberts. Since Hughes often voted with the liberals anyway, and since to him the maintenance of the prestige and influence of the Court was more significant than any economic theory, it was not difficult for him to come to the conclusion that liberalism was the order of the day. This left Roberts. What happened will possibly never be known, but Roberts performed the famous "switch in time that saved nine." Did Hughes use his influence? Did Roberts read the election returns and draw his own conclusions? Whatever happened, the great reversal on the Court came after the first of the year 1937. It came in several little-known cases first, then in the Wagner Act and succeeding New Deal issues.

This switch poses many questions, some of which were well presented in a leading journalistic account of the controversy:

When Hughes put this question to Roberts on the Wagner Act, was he already aware that the reply would approve the act's validity? Had he perhaps persuaded Roberts that to uphold a state minimum wage law was not enough, that the Court must allow the national government a free hand; and if he had, did he by any chance betray what had occurred by some brief alteration in his Olympian demeanor? Did the liberals allow themselves the wicked pleasure of hinting that much trouble might have been avoided if Roberts had voted with them from the start? Was McReynolds the only justice who seems to have wished the Court to die hard, openly infuriated? Above all, how did Roberts behave? Did he put his vote on the practical basis that circumstances had forced it on him? Or did he pass it off with legal explanation? Did he seem conscious that his switch would save the Court, or had he somehow rationalized it until he himself believed his course consistent? [26]

Whatever the answers, the shift came at the strategic time, and it was a permanent realignment; Roberts did not go back to conservatism until Roosevelt's appointees had given the New Deal a solid Court majority. The "Four Horsemen" continued to vote against almost all New Deal legislation, but they could now afford the luxury, for their votes no longer determined the issue. The matter was summed up by Thomas Reed Powell with a quotation from Fielding: "He . . . would have ravished her, if she had not, by a timely compliance, prevented him."

[26] Joseph Alsop and Turner Catledge, *The 168 Days* (Garden City: Double-day, Doran & Co., 1938), p. 143. Copyright 1937, 1938 by Joseph Alsop and Turner Catledge. Reprinted by permission of Doubleday and Company, Inc.

The Result

The reversal of the Supreme Court came in a series of dramatic 5 to 4 decisions which culminated in the approval of the Social Security Act,[27] the Wagner Labor Relations Act,[28] and a state minimum wage law (which involved the tacit reversal of the *Tipaldo Case*).[29] The importance of these decisions lay not only in the fact that important New Deal laws were upheld, but also in the implied reversal of previous New Deal cases. For the social security decision practically cut the ground from under the AAA opinion, and the Wagner Act case did the same for the NRA "sick chicken" case. Never again was the Court to disapprove of a New Deal law, even though some of them, especially the Fair Labor Standards Act,[30] went as far in the delegation of legislative power and in the control of interstate commerce as any of the previous laws that the Court had vetoed. The Court now entered a phase in which it was willing to allow a great deal of scope for legislative discretion, both at the national and state levels. The "self-restraint" for which Justice Stone had cried so eloquently became a fact. The Supreme Court revolution, then, consisted of the withdrawal of the Court from the field of economic and social legislation—its decision to refrain from judging the wisdom of such legislation or to let its "inarticulate major premises" dictate its constitutional opinions. Thus did the Supreme Court give up powers it had developed over a period of eighty years. Little wonder that the conservatives were aghast; McReynolds cried out in open court, "The Constitution is dead!" And it was true: the Constitution as Justices Butler, McReynolds, Van Devanter, and Sutherland knew it *was* dead.

Once more, then, the march of history had forced the Supreme Court and the Constitution to accommodate themselves to its changes. The Court again played the negative role which has been its chief function in the economic realm: it allowed new interpretations of the Constitution in an effort to adapt that ancient document to modern needs.

And what of President Roosevelt's court-packing bill? He refused to give it up for months, even though by mid-April it was certain that the bill would not pass. Finally, after the sudden death of his major spokesman in the Senate—Senator Joseph Robinson of Arkansas—the bill was dropped and a weak substitute measure, providing mainly for some renovations in the lower federal courts, was adopted. Thus, it has

---

[27] *Steward Machine Co.* v. *Davis*, 301 U.S. 548 (1937); *Helvering* v. *Davis*, 301 U.S. 619 (1937).

[28] *National Labor Relations Bd.* v. *Friedman-Harry Marks Clothing Co.*, 301 U.S. 58 (1937); *National Labor Relations Bd.* v. *Fruehauf Trailer Co.*, 301 U.S. 49 (1937); *National Labor Relations Bd.* v. *Jones & Laughlin Steel Corp.*, 301 U.S. 1 (1937).

[29] *West Coast Hotel Co.* v. *Parrish*, 300 U.S. 379 (1937).

[30] *United States* v. *Darby Lumber Co.*, 312 U.S. 100 (1941).

been said, the executive won the legal battle but the judges won the political battle. Roosevelt got what he was after: a changed attitude toward social and economic legislation. But the Court successfully forestalled the attempt to (as some charged) make it into an arm of the executive.

While the Court thus tacitly admitted defeat in the battle against the New Deal, it remains true that it gave up no actual powers. It remains possible that some future New Deal will have to undergo the same judicial scrutiny. At least theoretically, the power of judicial review is still held intact. There is, however, a good deal of doubt whether future justices will ever dare to use this weapon with any frequency. Judges are conscious of their limitations, and they can read history books. The lessons of 1937 are not likely soon to be forgotten, and the judges of the future are more likely to be oversophisticated about their function than overnaïve. In other words, the problem for the future will be to maintain *enough* of judicial review for the courts to play their proper role in safeguarding American constitutionalism. The record of the Court in civil liberties cases in the late 1940's and early 1950's was not encouraging in this respect, although the Court under Warren has been more active. The problem of the Supreme Court today is—as it has always been—the problem of using its powers enough to maintain constitutionalism but not so much as to defeat the necessities of government. And the danger is that the New Deal defeat made judges so alert to their proper limitations that they may no longer be willing to use their proper powers.

Roosevelt's Appointments and Their Course of Action

Justice Van Devanter's retirement gave President Roosevelt, after over four years in office, his first opportunity to place a man on the Supreme Court. It was a foregone conclusion that he would pick a New Dealer, or at the very least, a lower court judge with a liberal record. It seems possible that, smarting from his wounds in the court reform battle, and determined to make over the Court in the New Deal image, the President deliberately looked for the most rabid New Dealer he could find. He selected Senator Hugo Black of Alabama— a stalwart administration supporter and crusading liberal, who had made a reputation (which endeared him to liberals and fomented violent opposition among conservatives) by his slashing conduct of a Senate investigation into the activities of public utilities. Black had practiced law but had never been a judge except for a very brief stint as police judge in Birmingham. He was one of the authors of the very liberal Fair Labor Standards Act of 1938, which the Supreme Court later upheld with him as one of its members.

The political nature of Black's appointment is thus obvious even without recording the following conversation. Black asked the President, "Are you sure that I'll be more useful on the Court than in the Senate?" Roosevelt's reply was, "Hugo, I wish you were twins because Barkley says he needs you in the Senate; but I think you'll be more useful on the Court."

But it would not do to leave Black's appointment solely as a matter of administration politics. Tactically, it was considered wise to appoint a senator, for due to the traditional practices of that body it is almost impossible for it to refuse to confirm one of its own members. More important was the fact that Black was obviously an able man. The President—like most other chief executives—might want a political supporter on the bench, but he was not blind to the need of good men as judges. Incidentally, it is now generally conceded that the President was right, for in addition to being a liberal on the Court, Black has turned out to be a better-than-average jurist, and is often considered to be second only to Justice Frankfurter in his capacity as a judge.

That politics is important in Supreme Court appointments is made even more clear when one considers the nature of the opposition to Black's appointment. Many of those who had fought the court-packing proposal were horrified, for they had been fighting not only the proposal but to a large extent the New Deal itself. Yet here was the New Deal personified in the person of Hugo Black on the threshold of the Supreme Court. It was as if the Devil himself were trying to enter the Holy of Holies. Every possible objection to his appointment was dredged up. Since Van Devanter had retired instead of resigned, some said that there was no vacancy to fill. And of course most notorious was the matter of Black's previous membership in the Ku Klux Klan.

So, after a hard struggle, the New Deal entered the Supreme Court. After Black's appointment vacancies came thick and fast, and were invariably filled by New Dealers of varying degrees of enthusiasm and experience, so that by the time of Roosevelt's death only Stone and Roberts remained of the "old" Court. The seven New Dealers were, in addition to Black, Stanley Reed, a Kentuckian who had been general counsel for the Reconstruction Finance Corporation and then Solicitor General of the United States. He was appointed in 1938 to replace Justice Sutherland, and was a genial man of moderate opinions who made a creditable if not distinguished record. In 1939 Felix Frankfurter replaced Justice Cardozo, who died. Frankfurter is the most distinguished jurist and most controversial figure on the present Court. He came from a position as Dean of the Harvard Law School, where he had trained many who became not only New Deal lawyers but disciples of Frankfurter as well. His philosophy is Holmesian in its emphasis on objectivity. Politically, he was a New Dealer and one of Roosevelt's closest advisers. He is Jewish and maintains the tradition of having a Jew on the Court.

When Justice Brandeis resigned in 1939 his seat was taken by William O. Douglas, chairman of the Securities and Exchange Commission. Douglas has proved to be the real "crusader" of the Court, in this and other senses a fitting successor to Brandeis. He is a former Yale Law School professor, and was frequently charged with harboring presidential ambitions—a charge which was for some years abetted by regular booms for his name at Democratic national conventions.

In 1940 Frank Murphy, Attorney General, former Governor of Michigan and High Commissioner to the Philippines, took the place of Butler. Murphy was a Catholic from an important labor state and a strong civil libertarian and liberal. The last of the "Four Horsemen" to disappear was Justice McReynolds in 1941. The crusty conservative was succeeded by James F. Byrnes, senator from South Carolina since 1931—a man who, whatever his later reputation as a liberal, had supported the New Deal in Congress and had been a firm administration man.

Hughes's resignation in 1941 brought the elevation of Harlan Stone to the chief justiceship and the appointment of Robert H. Jackson to fill the vacancy. Jackson, like Murphy, was Attorney General at the time of his appointment. He was an ardent New Dealer who had written a powerful book criticizing the anti-New Deal decisions of the Court in its 1935 and 1936 terms. Justice Byrnes resigned in 1942 to become a presidential assistant in the conduct of the war, and was replaced by Wiley B. Rutledge, former dean of the Iowa University Law School, who was promoted from the Circuit Court of Appeals for the District of Columbia. Rutledge, though a liberal judge and justice, was the least "political" of any Roosevelt appointee so far as his background was concerned.

By the end of 1942, then, the Court consisted of seven Roosevelt appointees, the liberal Chief Justice Stone, and Justice Roberts. It can easily be seen that Roberts would be the "conservative wing" on such a Court, although having taken over the Court the New Dealers soon split among themselves. The new members were almost all "political lawyers" or practicing politicians, only Frankfurter—a "beneath the throne" politician—and Rutledge being exceptions. The point to be made is that Roosevelt, like almost every other President, was interested in securing "the right type of man" for service on the high court, and the right type of man was, as usual, judged at least partially from the political standpoint. Performing a political task, obviously, makes one a politician, and so all judges, regardless of previous experience, are politicians—but not in the same sense as presidents or legislators. The differences as well as the similarities have been explored in previous chapters.

Suggestions for Further Reading

Much of the literature about the "Supreme Court Revolution of 1937" is journalistic and not very reliable. In addition to the books listed below, there were innumerable magazine and law review articles published in the decade of the 1930's, which will not be listed here.

Perhaps the best book on this subject from a scholarly point of view is Dean Alfange's *The Supreme Court and the National Will* (Garden City: Doubleday, Doran & Co., 1937). The then Solicitor General, later Supreme Court justice, Robert H. Jackson, wrote a popular, New Deal oriented treatment, *The Struggle for Judicial Supremacy* (New York: Alfred A. Knopf, 1940). There are excellent overviews in the relevant sections of Charles P. Curtis, *Lions under the Throne* (Boston: Houghton Mifflin Co., 1947); C. Herman Pritchett, *The Roosevelt Court* (New York: The Macmillan Co., 1948); Merlo J. Pusey, *Charles Evans Hughes* (New York: The Macmillan Co., 1951); Alpheus T. Mason, *Harlan Fiske Stone: Pillar of the Law* (New York: The Viking Press, 1956); and Arthur M. Schlesinger, Jr., *The Politics of Upheaval* (Boston: Houghton Mifflin Co., 1960).

Journalistic accounts which may add interesting side lights are Joseph Alsop and Turner Catledge, *The 168 Days* (Garden City: Doubleday, Doran & Co., 1938); Drew Pearson and Robert S. Allen, *The Nine Old Men* (Garden City: Doubleday, Doran & Co., 1937); and Wesley McCune, *The Nine Young Men* (New York: Harper & Brothers, 1947).

Bernard Schwartz has dealt with the effects of the 1937 events in *The Supreme Court—Revolution in Retrospect* (New York: Ronald Press, 1957).

CHAPTER VII

Judicial Review
in Practice

*When the Court stands guard over any legal or economic theory, or
over the form of our governmental structure, they are taking a gamble
on the continuance of that theory, the outcome of which the Supreme
Court cannot be wise enough to predict. [History] . . . is spotted
with decisions declaring invalid unemployment insurance, income
taxes, federal employment agencies, railway pension schemes. None
of these decisions has turned back the stream of events. Each of them
has only added its quota of confusion.*

—THURMAN ARNOLD, *The Symbols of Government*

The American Constitution nowhere specifically gives the
Supreme Court the power of judicial review; yet, as we have seen, this
power is a vastly important one which has been used for many years.
Where did it come from? And, perhaps more important, what has been
the actual history of its use and how has it *in practice* affected the
course of events?

As to the origins of judicial review, one may turn both to the theory
and practice of government in England, the colonies, and the early
states; alternatively, one may search the implications of the Constitution itself. It is probable that the American adoption of such judicial
power came as a result of both; for even though John Marshall's
justification in *Marbury* v. *Madison* is couched almost entirely in terms
of the nature of the Constitution, it seems likely that historical ideas
and practices were equally influential.

131

Judicial Review: Its Background in English and Colonial Practice

Although it is true that the United States under the Constitution of 1789 was the first nation to institutionalize the device of judicial review, this does not mean that the delegates to the Convention in 1789 thought it up for themselves: they were largely innovators, but not inventors. The *idea* of judicial review was neither original nor new, and it had even been *practiced* on a few isolated (and, it must be conceded, somewhat doubtful) occasions in England (see Chapter I) and in the colonies. In addition, there were some other practices fairly well known to the framers which, while not constituting judicial review, nevertheless were suggestive of it. It will be helpful briefly to review these and to try to assess their influence.

One may cite first the activities of the British Privy Council which, sitting in London, provided in many cases an administrative review and disallowance of colonial actions. Further, there were a few cases in which the Privy Council actually seemed to be sitting as a court— as in, for instance, *Winthrop v. Lechmere,* a 1727 case in which the Privy Council declared that a Connecticut act abolishing the right of primogeniture was void as opposed to that colony's charter as well as to the common law.[1]

These Privy Council activities were not precisely judicial review; yet, as many commentators have pointed out, they quite possibly influenced the colonists by keeping before them the knowledge that their acts could be reviewed and even invalidated by a higher court. The Privy Council also in some cases acted as a court of appeals to which regular legal cases might be appealed by the colonists themselves. Here again the idea of a supreme judicial body to dispose finally of their cases was present.

There were also a few cases in which colonial courts attempted to invalidate acts of Parliament or of their colonial assemblies. However, none of the devices so far mentioned can be regarded as having been directly influential in the adoption of judicial review. Possibly more significant was the existence of the colonial charters. For these came to be regarded as fundamental laws antedating and superior to the colonial governments: they had thus some of the status of a constitution. Colonists were in the habit of appealing to charter provisions. And insofar as the charters were private corporate charters—as in Pennsylvania—they were construed, and governmental acts under them could be set aside by ordinary judicial processes. The colonists thus became very familiar with the idea of judicial interpretation of their charters; and since the charters were, in some sense, constitutional

---

[1] *Winthrop v. Lechmere* (1727). See Homer C. Hockett, *Constitutional History of the United States, 1776–1826* (New York: The Macmillan Co., 1939), pp. 55–56.

documents, it was not unnatural that this attitude carried over to the Constitution when it was adopted.

Colonial and revolutionary statesmen had some concept of judicial review—vague as it may have been—as the reference to James Otis in Chapter I indicates. They could also appeal—wrongly, it may be—to Lord Coke's famous dictum in *Dr. Bonham's Case*, in which he seemed to say that an act of Parliament in conflict with the common law is void.[2]

Judicial Review in the Early State Governments

The use of judicial review became somewhat more definite in the early state governments during the years of 1776–1789. There are many statements showing that statesmen of the period were familiar with judicial review. That of George Wythe, possibly the most famous lawyer of his day and the teacher of Jefferson and Marshall, may be cited as representative. Sitting as a Virginia state judge, Wythe declared:

. . . [I]f the whole legislature . . . should attempt to overleap the bounds prescribed to them by the people, I in administering the public justice of the country will meet the united powers, at my seat in this tribunal; and, pointing to the constitution, will say to them, here is the limit of your authority; and hither shall you go, but no further.[3]

Perhaps the clearest instance of judicial review in a case during this period was *Bayard* v. *Singleton*, in which the court stated the principle in these words:

. . . [I]t was clear, that no act they [the legislature] could pass could by any means repeal or alter the constitution, because if they could do this, they would at the same instant of time destroy their own existence as a Legislature, and dissolve the government thereby established. Consequently the constitution (which the judicial power was bound to take notice of as much as of any other law whatever), standing in full force as the fundamental law of the land, notwithstanding the act on which the present motion was grounded, the same act must, of course, in the instance, stand as abrogated and without any effect.[4]

This argument was ably supported by James Iredell—a counsel in the case and a future Supreme Court justice—both in the case being discussed and in letters to friends.

There is, thus, no doubt that judicial review was known to and approved by many revolutionary statesmen, and even applied in a few instances. While these applications were neither numerous nor unchallenged, they do indicate a familiarity with the principle.

[2] *Dr. Bonham's Case*, 8 Coke's Reports 114a (1610).
[3] *Commonwealth* v. *Caton*, 4 Call (Va.) 5 (1782).
[4] *Bayard* v. *Singleton*, 1 Martin (N.C.) 42 (1787).

Judicial Review in the Constitution

The available records of the Constitutional Convention do not tell whether the framers intended judicial review to be embodied in the Constitution; any such embodiment must be gleaned therefore from vague constitutional phraseology, from statements made by delegates, or (as Marshall later did) from "the nature of a written Constitution." Such men as Elbridge Gerry, Luther Martin, Rufus King, James Wilson, Oliver Ellsworth, and James Madison expressed ideas favoring judicial review. C. C. Pinckney, James Mercer, John Dickinson, and Benjamin Franklin, among others, expressed opposition. Little can be proved by attempting to determine the intentions of the framers. It seems at least possible, however, that they may have felt it impolitic to write such a novel proposition, to which there was much opposition, explicitly into the Constitution. They may well have thought that review would be asserted by the courts even without such an express grant of the power; and anyway many of them may have felt that judicial review, like the separation of powers, was a fundamental part of any republican form of government whether or not the doctrine was expressly stated.

In the state conventions on the ratification of the Constitution, similarly varied interpretations were made. John Marshall expressed his views favoring the power in the Virginia Convention, as did Hamilton in New York (and in *The Federalist*, No. 78), Sam Adams in Massachusetts, and others. But Edmund Randolph, George Mason, and Richard Henry Lee opposed it in Virginia.

The Judiciary Act of 1789 may indirectly express a belief in judicial review. Yet, when all is said, the evidence is at best circumstantial. All that can be said with certainty is that the idea of judicial review was not unknown to the framers and that some of them favored its use. The general political philosophy of the period, with its emphasis on written constitutions as fundamental law and on natural rights, seems to lead rather naturally to judicial review: even its greatest opponents, Madison and Jefferson, at one time favored it. As Professor Benjamin F. Wright has said, "the ultimate origins of this institution are part of the seamless web of history."

The Supreme Court and Judicial Review: Early Cases

Haines cites eleven state cases between the adoption of the Constitution and the *Marbury Case* in which judicial review was used.[5] However, one need not regard these as precedents for federal court action in any direct sense: again, the most they do is indicate that this power of courts was not unknown either in theory or practice. What is

[5] Charles Grove Haines, *The American Doctrine of Judicial Supremacy* (New York: The Macmillan Co., 1914).

not so often remarked is that the Supreme Court itself had at least once assumed that it had the power to invalidate federal laws prior to 1803, and that the justices on circuit had several times done the same. This occurred in the *Hylton Case* in 1796;[6] the case of *Calder v. Bull* applied the same idea as to state laws in 1798.[7] However, in neither case did the Court find the law unconstitutional. The importance of the cases lies in the fact that *the Court accepted jurisdiction* and that several judges explicitly admitted they would rule the laws void if they thought them violative of the Constitution. The Supreme Court, in other words, assumed the power to declare legislation invalid before it actually used the power affirmatively. In actuality federal judicial review begins not in 1803, but in 1796 or even earlier.

Marbury v. *Madison*[8]

The celebrated "Case of the Midnight Judges" in 1803 was the first case in which the Court clearly found a piece of legislation unconstitutional. This fact makes it probably the leading case in American constitutional law. It is not made less interesting by the fact that it was a "political" case, or by the accident that it directly involved several leading American heroes—Jefferson and John Adams in addition to Madison and Marshall. The case thus deserves—indeed, requires—extended consideration.

The election of 1800 was a Federalist disaster: the "Jeffersonian revolution" seemed to bode ill to Federalist leaders. As the news of the election results spread through staunchly conservative New England towns, bells of mourning were rung in Congregationalist churches in grief at the passing of the Republic. The leveling Jacobin, Jefferson, had become President. Surely no worse disaster could befall America. The democrats—Fisher Ames called them "democratick babblers"—would now proceed to destroy the rights of property and erect King Numbers as sovereign.

In such an atmosphere Federalists naturally took thought to preserve their dominance wherever they could. What better place than the judiciary, independent and life-tenured, which Hamilton had earlier envisaged as the bulwark of propertied interests? Therefore Federalist leaders set about the task of creating and maintaining a Federalist judiciary and of turning the Supreme Court from an insignificant body, for which it was even difficult to recruit judges, into a powerful protective agency. There was substance to Jefferson's charge that the Federalists retired into the judiciary, there to erect a battlement to defeat democratic policies.

---

[6] *Hylton* v. *United States*, 3 Dallas 171 (1796).
[7] *Calder* v. *Bull*, 3 Dallas 386 (1798).
[8] *Marbury* v. *Madison*, 1 Cranch 137 (1803).

"In the desire," as Professor Haines says, "to keep the fountain of justice pure and uncontaminated by the waters of Republicanism," [9] the Federalists during their "lame duck" session of Congress in early 1801 enacted three laws: one reducing the size of the Supreme Court from six to five, in the hope of preventing Jefferson from appointing a Republican to the Court; another creating an indeterminate number of justice of the peace positions for the District of Columbia; and a third creating sixteen circuit judgeships. All positions, of course, were to be filled with deserving Federalists. President John Adams thereupon designated forty-two men for the justice of the peace positions; the nominations were approved by the Senate on March 3, 1801—the day before Jefferson was to take office. Legend has Adams staying up late that night signing the commissions of the designated persons. It is certain that his Secretary of State, one John Marshall (just confirmed as the new Chief Justice of the Supreme Court) failed to deliver the commissions—Marshall pleaded lack of time and personnel—so that the commissions were still in the Secretary's office when Jefferson's appointee, James Madison, took over. None was delivered. William Marbury and three others thereupon applied to the Supreme Court, in an original action under Section 13 of the Judiciary Act of 1789, for a writ of mandamus to compel Madison to deliver the commissions, claiming that Adams' signature completed the necessary legal steps and that they therefore had a right to the commissions.

The Republicans, for their part, had no love for the Federalist Supreme Court; it had been both intemperate and violently partisan in jury charges and general conduct in enforcing the Alien and Sedition Acts of 1798, which had tried to silence the outspoken and often scurrilous Republican attacks on the Adams administration. Chief Justice Ellsworth, for instance, had denounced the Jeffersonians in no mincing words, calling them "apostles of atheism, anarchy, bloodshed, and plunder." Republicans therefore, as soon as they entered office, tried to mitigate Federalist control of the judiciary. They restored the Court to its original size (seven), giving Jefferson an immediate opportunity to appoint a new justice; abolished the circuit court positions the Federalists had created; and changed the provisions for the Washington justices of the peace. Then, to prevent the Supreme Court from declaring the action as to the circuit courts unconstitutional, they changed the term of the Court from June and December (1802) to one February term. This meant that the Supreme Court did not meet from December, 1801 (before the passage of the Republican legislation), until February of 1803. Therefore Marbury's case was not decided until two years after Jefferson took office.

There are numerous interesting angles about the *Marbury Case.*

---

[9] Charles Grove Haines, *The Role of the Supreme Court in American Government and Politics* (Berkeley: University of California Press, 1944), p. 245.

Not the least of these centers around the question of whether Marshall —a personal participant in the events leading to the case—could ethically act as a judge in the litigation. Suffice it to say that partisan feelings ran high and Marshall's partisanship was stronger than his sense of judicial propriety. It might also be fair to add that the judicial code of ethics was much less highly developed in 1803 than it is today. In any case, Marshall not only sat in the case but wrote the opinion, which was a masterly political and legal stroke despite its many technical deficiencies.

Marshall and the Supreme Court faced a difficult choice. They could issue the writ of mandamus for which Marbury had applied, but it was certain that Jefferson and Madison would ignore it—thus further damaging the already low prestige of the Court. On the other hand, it would be a denial of their Federalist partisanship to hold that Marbury and his fellows had no right to the commissions. A more obvious possibility was to refuse to accept the case on grounds of lack of jurisdiction; but to do so would give Jefferson complete victory without even a battle.

John Marshall, a superb constitutional tactician, did neither of these things. He contrived simultaneously to castigate the Jefferson administration for failure to observe its legal duties; to admit that Marbury had a right to his commission yet to deny him the writ; and—at the same time—to claim and establish for his Court a broad power of judicial review far beyond the requirements of the case! Let us follow the course of his reasoning.

First, Marshall considered (not the Court's jurisdiction, which in most cases is the initial question) whether Marbury had a right to the commission. He deduced that the President's signature and the seal of the Secretary of State were all that were needed to make a commission valid; delivery of the commission to the appointee was not a necessary part of the process. Consequently Marbury had a right to the commission and the job.

Next Marshall asked, is there a legal remedy for the wrong perpetrated by Madison? He invoked Blackstone's dictum that there is a legal remedy for every legal right; and, legally, the government must therefore deliver the commission. However, he went on, the particular remedy Marbury asked for (a writ of mandamus), while it is a proper legal remedy, is not within the power of the Supreme Court to issue. Why? Because the *original jurisdiction* of the Supreme Court is defined in the Constitution: this definition is exclusive, and does not include the mandamus power. The power to issue such writs stems from Section 13 of the Judiciary Act of 1789; but since Congress has no power to add to the original jurisdiction of the Court, Section 13 is unconstitutional.

The question then remained whether the Supreme Court could exercise a jurisdiction unlawfully conferred upon it. Marshall had to answer "no," both because of his beliefs and due to the political necessities of the case. This being so, he had two alternatives. First, he could limit the statement of the principle of judicial review by confining it to cases involving the judicial power. This would have accomplished one of his purposes, and would have been consistent with the separation of powers idea that each branch of the government should interpret the extent of its own powers.

Second, Marshall could enunciate the theory of judicial review in terms broad enough to cover all types of governmental acts, both national and state. Probably because of his ambitions for the Court, and in the hope that a powerful Federalist Court could secure some nationalistic policies, he chose the second alternative.

It remains merely to mention Marshall's line of argument as to the powers of the Supreme Court. He quoted no constitutional clauses, cited no precedents, mentioned no speeches from the Constitutional Convention. He rested his case entirely on his view of the *logic* of a written Constitution—just as Hamilton had done in *The Federalist*, No. 78, and (not improbably) as the framers had done in omitting specific mention of the doctrine. In Corwin's words, "We are driven to the conclusion that judicial review was rested . . . upon certain general principles which in their estimation made specific provision for it unnecessary." [10]

While the *Marbury Case* occasioned a great political outcry, not even Jefferson criticized it for the Court's assumption of judicial review powers: all the criticism was aimed at Marshall's temerity in lecturing the administration. The doctrine of judicial review thus slipped into American constitutional practice almost unnoticed. But for all that, the *Marbury Case* has served as an effective precedent.

The Supreme Court and Judicial Review: Succeeding Cases

Not again for over fifty years was a federal act to be invalidated by the Supreme Court. It is important to note, nevertheless, that from 1796 on, there was a steady stream of cases in which the constitutionality of federal acts was considered; so far as is known, no federal judge, and no lawyer at the federal bar, ever challenged its use. Judicial review, apparently, fitted the national political temper so ideally that this one case of its practice was enough to place it beyond effective challenge. As it happened, conditions were such that not until the *Dred Scott Case* in 1857 did the Supreme Court feel called upon to invalidate another act—in this instance one that had already been superseded by a later Congressional act. But as numerous cases il-

---

[10] Edward S. Corwin, *The Doctrine of Judicial Review* (Princeton: Princeton University Press, 1914), p. 17.

lustrate—such as *McCulloch* v. *Maryland* [11]—constitutionality was a question the Court was always ready to consider.

Judicial Review and State Action

The *Marbury Case* settled the issue of judicial review so far as federal acts were concerned, but it was not until 1810 that the Supreme Court used the power to invalidate a *state* act. However, as in the case of federal acts, there had previously been cases in court—such as *Calder* v. *Bull*—in which the constitutionality of a state act was the principal issue. The Court had not declined to hear such cases, but had invariably ruled in favor of the state. *Fletcher* v. *Peck*[12] thus becomes the first real precedent for judicial review of state acts. (State judicial decisions involving the federal Constitution constitute a separate class of cases, in which the Supreme Court earlier assumed jurisdiction.)

Fletcher v. *Peck*, too, was bound up in economic and political considerations; its origins go back at least to 1795, and several Court justices and other leading politicians were either involved in it or interested in its outcome. Again, this case illustrates well the political implications of court decisions.

In 1789 Georgia began attempts to sell the Yazoo lands (now comprising most of Alabama and Mississippi) to private land companies. The sale, however, was not consummated until 1795, when the legislature granted huge tracts to the land companies under conditions of wholesale bribery and corruption. Supreme Court Justice James Wilson was one of the investors, as were other prominent statesmen; and in a larger sense, land speculation was a fad of the times for those with money to invest, as stock market speculation became in the 1920's. Consequently, all those interested in land disposal—a category which included even Marshall himself—were intimately concerned with the outcome of the Yazoo land question. The state hoped to open up the land for settlement; the speculators hoped to make money by reselling the land at a profit. Indeed, having paid $500,000 to Georgia, the companies are said to have realized $1,000,000 *in profits* through the resale of eleven million acres the very day the law was passed!

The public outcry in Georgia was tremendous, and the next election saw the defeat of most of the legislators who had been responsible. The new legislature immediately proceeded to repeal the grant. The companies, however, disregarded the repeal, and both speculators and buyers continued to transfer the land. Land was sold to actually innocent purchasers as well as to persons in collusion with the speculators. In 1802 Georgia ceded the whole territory to the United States.

---

[11] *McCulloch* v. *Maryland*, 4 Wheaton 316 (1819).
[12] *Fletcher* v. *Peck*, 6 Cranch 87 (1810).

The question then naturally arose whether the United States was bound to recognize title to land held by the so-called "innocent purchasers"—anyone who had bought land from companies or from later buyers. In a test case, finally, Robert Fletcher bought a small piece of land from John Peck, then sued him to get his money back on the claim that Peck had fraudulently sold him land to which he did not have title.

The technicalities of the Supreme Court decision are not of great interest here; at this point it is only of importance to note that the Court found Georgia's rescinding act an unconstitutional treatment of the contract clause. The effect was to validate the title of all the later purchasers of the land involved, regardless of the corruption which occurred in the original grant. Marshall's motives had to do with the defense of the property right, which, as a good Federalist, he regarded as fundamental to society. The most independent Jeffersonian on the Court—William Johnson—dissented (in part).

In such a political and economic context, then, was the power of the Supreme Court over state legislation first used. As in the *Marbury Case*, the controversy over the decision concerned its immediate effects, not its assertion of a hitherto only speculative power.

The review of state acts was naturally more frequent than that of actions of the national government. Nevertheless, it is true that up until the Civil War, the power was used rather sparingly, principally in contract clause cases in which (under Marshall) the Court was protecting vested property rights, and (under Taney) commerce clause cases involving a conflict between state and national authority, but still with rights of private property a basic consideration.

The Expansion of Government, 1870–1935

The number of times that legislation has been found unconstitutional shows a definite periodicity in United States history. Such findings were made, as we have seen, infrequently from 1790 until after the Civil War. Beginning about 1870, however, their frequency greatly increased both in federal and state legislation. This striking increase continued until 1937, but has in the last twenty years declined almost as remarkably as it rose in the 1870's. Thus American history provides one rather long period of judicial activity sandwiched between periods of relative quiescence. Our concern at this point is to explain this variation.

The importance of the Supreme Court as a decision-making body in vital areas of social and economic policy has been stressed heretofore in this book. It has also been pointed out that normally the courts are conservative and negative rather than liberal and initiative. It follows that judicial review will be used most often in periods when the American governments are striking out into new and hitherto unknown areas of activity. If this is true it explains much of the variation pointed to above.

In the years before the Civil War the United States was a growing country. But its growth was predominantly territorial and agricultural. Government remained largely within the areas of traditional governmental activities. The dominant form of property was land, and its protection was a matter of such consensus that government seldom interfered. It is notable, even so, that most of the cases of judicial review involved property interests, as in *Fletcher* v. *Peck* and the *Dred Scott Case*,[13] in which land and slave property were involved, and in *Gibbons* v. *Ogden*,[14] in which corporate property was a leading factor. But on the whole government was concerned with traditional areas such as maintaining peace and order.

The industrial revolution changed all this. The United States entered upon a period of a tremendous industrial expansion—an expansion which in its process completely changed American society. Agriculture gave way to industry, rural life to urban, land ownership to corporate property. And, particularly in its earlier stages, this drastic upheaval brought many evils and much hardship to some groups. The cry went up from these groups for government protection. And our government, as democratic governments must, gave heed to the cries. First the state governments and then the national government began to legislate to protect some groups and to regulate others. All of this new legislation interfered with the free conduct of the newly predominant property interest—the corporation. In self-defense corporate interests turned to the courts. The often fumbling attempts of government to cope with radically new social and economic conditions were frequently challenged in court and often blocked by courts using both old and new doctrines of constitutional interpretation, chief among them the commerce clause and substantive due process. This continued, as we have seen, through the early years of the New Deal.

Why did the courts lend themselves to such a process? Partly, no doubt, due to the conservative nature of law in general and the common law in particular. Beyond this, the fact is that the judges were often self-made men, and men who in addition had served as counsel to the same interests they were later called upon to defend. These factors perhaps led them to share the attitudes of the business community. The long succession of Republican presidents, broken only three times from 1860 to 1932, ensured the predominance of Republican views on the Court. The decisions invalidating government action were largely in the economic realm and, as Professor Wright has pointed out, they were very largely the product of the Court's reluctance to accept the consequences of the industrial revolution.[15]

---

[13] *Scott* v. *Sandford*, 19 Howard 393 (1857).
[14] *Gibbons* v. *Ogden*, 9 Wheaton 1 (1824).
[15] Benjamin F. Wright, *The Growth of American Constitutional Law* (New York: Henry Holt & Co., 1942), p. 256.

Judicial political activism is always a potential consequence of judicial review. But it is likely to remain latent except in periods of rapid governmental expansion into new areas. During such an era it may burst into frequent use, until such time as the courts catch up to the rest of the government—which happens partly because of the accession of new judges and partly because governmental expansion after a period of activity usually slows down.

To put the matter somewhat differently, it might be said that judicial review tends to seize upon the restrictive possibilities of the Constitution when the *status quo* is rapidly changing; whereas at other times —when change is slow and piecemeal—it is more likely to allow the use of the Constitution's expansive possibilities. The Court is thus a brake which comes most fully into use when society is traveling fast.

Judicial Review since 1937

After 1937 two principal factors combined to produce a rapid decline in the use of judicial review. In the first place, as the discussion of Roosevelt's clash with the Supreme Court demonstrated, the Court caught up with the New Deal because the weight of events and the appointment of new justices forced it to. Second, and perhaps not less important, the pace of government activity lessened and its focus shifted. The New Deal had almost ended by 1938; the war came a year later and took the center of the political stage; prosperity and conservatism came in its wake. Consequently, only four relatively minor federal acts have been found invalid since 1936, and the state cases have correspondingly declined.

But equally important is the fact that the Court no longer regards itself as an economic censor: it now proceeds on the assumption that the Constitution imposes no particular economic theory on the American people. There is likely to be no repetition of the 1870–1937 era of judicial activity except in some noneconomic area of governmental activity such as civil rights or liberties. The economic aspects of substantive due process seem dead.

As a matter of fact, the principal area of judicial activity since World War II has been that of civil rights and liberties, and peculiarly enough judicial decisions in these areas have embroiled the Court in controversy as heated as that of the New Deal era. This has led to another "great debate" about the proper role of the Court in our system of government and to renewed charges that it is "legislating," that it is "political," and that it is weakening the position of the states in the federal system.

It is one of history's little ironies that some of the very men who criticized the Court in the 1920's and 1930's for its excessive activism are now—as judges or commentators—engaged in defending it against similar charges. And it is significant that the judges of the Supreme

Court, unanimous though they were in scrapping the "old" Court's attitudes toward business regulation and social legislation, have split nine ways on the question of how the Court should act when civil liberties questions come before it. Justice Felix Frankfurter was one of the great critics of the Court when he was Dean of the Harvard Law School and a writer for the *New Republic,* and he has drawn from the story of the New Deal the moral that the Court should *never* (well, hardly ever) be activist. Thus he is very reluctant to use the power of judicial review to strike down state or federal action even in the field of civil liberties; he obviously feels that this is consistent with his earlier position, and that it allows due deference to the actions of legislatures as representatives of the people.

On the other hand, Justice Hugo Black, one of the New Deal Senate leaders, and Justice William O. Douglas, a Roosevelt administrative appointee, have concluded that there is such a vast difference between the issues presented by the New Deal cases and those presented in modern civil liberties cases that a judge is justified in treating them differently. They point to the fact that civil liberties are a necessity to a democracy and to the Constitution's express prohibition of their abridgment as justifications for judicial activism in this area.

There is logic in both positions, and, perhaps fortunately, both have had their influence on the actual line of Court decisions. For a Court without any Black or Douglas might provide no protection at all for civil liberties, while a Court with no Frankfurter might protect them at the cost of its own existence or prestige—and fail in the long run to achieve real protection.

In any event, the questions of race discrimination, of freedom of speech and religion, of control of subversive activities, and other issues of similar nature have come in the last twenty years to occupy the important place in constitutional jurisprudence which was once filled by questions of the proper scope of the commerce clause and the application of due process to the protection of business from state regulation. As the nature of the great issues of politics has changed, the nature of the great issues coming before the Court has also changed. The great domestic political issues still come to the Court, of course, as always, transmuted into legal controversies. And as a consequence, whatever may have been thought late in 1937, the Supreme Court has not retired from the politico-constitutional battleground; on the contrary, it is just as powerful today, and judicial review is just as important as ever.

The Effects of Judicial Review on American History

To what extent has the existence of judicial review affected the course of history? Opinions on this question vary considerably. On the one hand are those who, like Thurman Arnold (see chapter headnote), believe that our history would be about the same even if there had been no Supreme Court. To Arnold, judicial review has added "confusion" to history but has not changed it.

On the other hand, there are observers—both liberal and conservative—who believe the Court has been a dominant factor in our history. Liberals, until recently, tended to regard this effect as baneful, while conservatives thought of it as beneficial. Thus, the liberal Louis Boudin has called the Supreme Court a "great governmental agency pervading and controlling every department of our life," and has said further, that "the *general* character of our government is determined by the *class* or *type* of men who administer it under the Judicial Power." [16] The conservative Charles Warren arrives at the same conclusion:

> No one can read the history of the Court's career without marveling at its potent effect on the political development of the Nation, and without concluding that the Nation owes most of its strength to the determination of the Judges to maintain the National supremacy.[17]

It seems likely that the Boudin-Warren view overestimates, as the Arnold view underestimates, the importance of judicial review. Both views are, of course, based on historical guesswork, since no one can be sure what would have happened had any particular historical event not occurred. But additionally, each view presents an unbalanced approach to history. It would be difficult to gainsay that decisions such as those in *Gibbons* v. *Ogden*,[18] the *Dred Scott Case*,[19] the *Slaughterhouse Cases*,[20] or the *Sugar Trust Case*[21] had a pronounced effect on United States history. True, the effect cannot be measured, but its imponderable nature does not deny its existence. It would be just as difficult, however, to interpret all United States history in the light of Court activities, as does Boudin. This view ignores salient facts—particularly the fact that many important uses of judicial review have been overruled by the course of later events. But we have also introduced a major qualification: that there are times when the Court may actually be *ahead* of public opinion, as it was in Marshall's nationalistic opinions. In such cases not only does the Court's decision stand, but it becomes one of the factors *shaping* the dominant opinions of the public. The Court is neither the dominant power in government nor is it powerless.

Many theories have been used to explain the Court's position.

---

[16] Louis Boudin, *Government by Judiciary* (2 vols.; New York: William Godwin, Inc., 1932), Vol. II, p. 545.

[17] Charles Warren, *The Supreme Court in United States History* (Boston: Little, Brown & Co., 1937), Vol. I, p. vii.

[18] *Supra.*

[19] *Supra.*

[20] *Slaughterhouse Cases*, 16 Wallace 36 (1873).

[21] *United States* v. *E. C. Knight Co.*, 156 U.S. 1 (1895).

Professor Earl Latham, for instance, believes that the Court is powerful when (as in the due process cases in the period 1890–1930) it has support from large and strong interest groups, but that it is weak when (as in the civil liberties cases in 1945–50) no powerful social group comes to its support.[22]

Probably the most accurate summation of the historical role of the Court and of judicial review would take such theories as Latham's into account. In so doing, the conclusion seems to be that the Court is most important as a delaying agent, which forces the mobilization of substantial and relatively stable majorities before unprecedented actions can be taken.

One note of uncertainty needs to be added: no one knows how influential the *threat* of the use of judicial review may be. It does not complete the analysis to point out how few the occasions of its exercise have been, for the very existence of the power may condition governmental acts. No direct evidence on this point is available; such evidence as there is, however, suggests that the threat of the judicial veto is psychological and subconscious rather than conscious and overt. Review probably conditions the general attitudes of government officialdom rather than its views on specific questions. Within this area, the threat is doubtless of some importance.

The conclusion of this analysis, as suggested above, is that the Supreme Court has perhaps not basically been a determinative agency in the *general direction* of our history, but within that general direction it has very probably helped to shape specific trends in specific areas. And in some cases it has held back—temporarily—or facilitated our progress in these "general directions."

Suggestions for Further Reading

Judicial Review: Its Background in English and Colonial Practice

The works of Charles H. McIlwain, cited in the notes to Chapters I and II, are most useful for the English background. As to the colonial period, see Edward S. Corwin, *The Doctrine of Judicial Review* (Princeton: Princeton University Press, 1914); Charles G. Haines, *The American Doctrine of Judicial Supremacy* (New York: The Macmillan Co., 1932); Frank R. Strong, *American Constitutional Law* (Buffalo: Dennis & Co., 1950); and, for a dissenting view, Louis B. Boudin, *Government by Judiciary* (New York: William Godwin, Inc., 1932), Vol. I.

---

[22] Earl Latham, "The Supreme Court and the Supreme People," *Journal of Politics*, XVI, No. 2 (May, 1954), 207.

Judicial Review in the Early State Governments

All the works cited immediately above are useful here as well. There is also a good summary in Volume I of Homer C. Hockett's *Constitutional History of the United States* (New York: The Macmillan Co., 1939).

Judicial Review in the Constitution

Many of the books cited for Chapter II are relevant here, as well as those listed above. See also W. W. Crosskey's iconoclastic *Politics and the Constitution in the History of the United States* (Chicago: University of Chicago Press, 1953), Vol. I; Charles Warren, *The Supreme Court in United States History* (Boston: Little, Brown & Co., 1928); Charles L. Black, *The People and the Court* (New York: The Macmillan Co., 1960); and Ralph L. Ketcham, "James Madison and Judicial Review," 8 *Syracuse Law Rev.* 158 (1957).

The Use of Judicial Review in American History

Many works treat this subject in varying detail. Some of the more useful ones are listed here. Those by Warren, Crosskey, and Boudin, cited above, should be added to the list.

Cahn, Edmond (ed.). *Supreme Court and Supreme Law* (Bloomington: Indiana University Press, 1954).

Corwin, Edward S. *John Marshall and the Constitution* (New Haven: Yale University Press, 1919).

Haines, Charles G. *The Role of the Supreme Court in American Government and Politics, 1789–1835* (Berkeley: University of California Press, 1944).

————, and Sherwood, Foster H. *The Role of the Supreme Court in American Government and Politics, 1835–1864* (Berkeley: University of California Press, 1957).

Kelly, Alfred H., and Harbison, W. A. *The American Constitution* (New York: W. W. Norton, 1948).

Latham, Earl. "The Supreme Court and the Supreme People," 16 *Jnl. of Politics* 207 (1954).

McBain, Howard L. *The Living Constitution* (New York: The Macmillan Co., 1927).

McCloskey, Robert G. *The American Supreme Court* (Chicago: University of Chicago Press, 1960).

McLaughlin, Andrew C. *Constitutional History of the United States* (New York: D. Appleton & Co., 1935).

Mason, Alpheus T. *The Supreme Court from Taft to Warren* (Baton Rouge: Louisiana State University Press, 1956).

Mendelson, Wallace. *Capitalism, Democracy and the Supreme Court* (New York: Appleton-Century-Crofts, 1960).

Read, Conyers (ed.). *The Constitution Reconsidered* (New York: Columbia University Press, 1938).

Rodell, Fred. *Nine Men: A Political History of the Supreme Court of the United States from 1790 to 1955* (New York: Random House, 1955).

Rottschaefer, Henry. *The Constitution and Socio-Economic Change* (Ann Arbor: University of Michigan Law School, 1948).

Schwartz, Bernard. *American Constitutional Law* (Cambridge: Cambridge University Press, 1955).

Swisher, Carl B. *The Growth of Constitutional Power in the United States* (Chicago: University of Chicago Press, 1946).

————. *American Constitutional Development* (2d ed., Boston: Houghton Mifflin Co., 1954).

Wright, Benjamin F. *The Growth of American Constitutional Law* (New York: Reynal & Hitchcock, 1942).

CHAPTER VIII

The Supreme Court
and the
American Polity

*Can we wish governmental functions on a law court and yet insist
that it remain nothing but a law court?*

—CHARLES P. CURTIS, *Lions under the Throne*

The place of the Supreme Court in the American political
system is, as we have seen, somewhat anomalous. It is, on the one
hand, a court of law, using the procedures and (to a large extent)
the habits of thought common to courts of law. It decides legal cases
in a legal way. It is important to keep in mind, in this connection,
that many of the things the Supreme Court does must be done in any
legal system: it is always necessary to interpret the laws which the
courts are to apply, and it is everywhere the practice to have superior
courts review the decisions of lower courts. In performing such necessary tasks, the Supreme Court is different only in degree from courts
in Great Britain or any of the countries using the common law
system; and it is different only in somewhat greater degree from
courts anywhere in the world. What makes the United States Supreme Court different from most other courts is the power of judicial
review of governmental acts. And it is this same power which creates
the anomaly. For while the Court in constitutional cases is *in form*
doing the same thing it does in nonconstitutional issues—that is, it
is deciding what the law is—nevertheless *in substance* it is doing
something with far broader and more important direct and indirect

political implications. The "legalness" of Supreme Court decisions is thus, to some extent, a façade.

What we Americans have done, by inventing judicial review, is to force our courts and judges to play a political role. And this role is not the less political because we can justify it in legal or constitutional terms, as was done in the first two chapters of this book. Two specific difficulties stand in the way of courts acting merely as legal instruments when they deal with constitutional issues. Both of these have been canvassed thoroughly in this book: one is the fact that the law to be interpreted is the Constitution—a document that speaks to a twentieth-century world in an eighteenth-century voice, and that is perhaps deliberately vague and general to begin with; the second is the fact that constitutional issues coming to the Court are only incidentally legal or constitutional in nature, being primarily arguments over political, social, or economic questions of great import to our polity. Thus issues come to the judges burdened with the emotional and moral content—not to mention the ever-present question of what is the *rational* thing to do in a given situation—which always envelops great political issues. Even at best, one could not expect judges to divest themselves of their own emotional and moral feelings, so that they could act as political eunuchs guarding the constitutional seraglio. And the ambiguity of the Constitution ensures that the judges never can work under the best circumstances: the Constitution is so ambiguous that there is always reasonable doubt that the inhabitants of the harem really want to be guarded.

Thus it is natural and probably inevitable that Supreme Court decisions partake of the humanity which invests all human institutions, and that, in fact, our system gives greater play to this humanity than judges are normally allowed in other societies. We may not consciously desire or expect judicial decisions to be politically oriented; we merely force them to be. In this context the difference between so-called "humilitarian" judges who preach and practice judicial self-restraint is a difference of degree only from those "activists" who believe they should use judicial review to remold the world closer to their heart's desire. For all are equally using their own interpretations of constitutionality, and, in a way, all are using these interpretations to secure the kind of constitutional universe they believe in. Holmes and Frankfurter, for all their belief in self-restraint, are thus brothers under the skin to Sutherland and Black.

This is not to say that our history would be the same if the alignments on the Court in any period had been different. The actual decisions of the Court are shaped partly by direct public opinion and partly by the ideas of the men occupying the bench. If these men were different men, it follows that some decisions would be somewhat different. A Court made up of Frankfurters would not have outlawed the requirement of the salute to the flag in public schools;[1] and a Court consisting of Blacks would not have upheld prior censorship of movies.[2] These decisions were in areas in which decisions either way were politically and legally feasible; whereas no Court regardless of personnel could have struck down the law prohibiting polygamy in the 1870's.[3] Courts work within a framework of possibilities; they can go outside the framework (which is formed by public opinion) only at the peril of destroying their court or its role. But within the framework they are relatively free, as the cases referred to in various parts of this book have illustrated.

What may be contended, however, is that the great American debate of recent years over the proper role of the Supreme Court in civil rights and liberties cases has misconceived the real point at issue. Most argument has concerned whether the courts should exercise self-restraint in this as in other fields: Justice Frankfurter has stood as the exemplar of this point of view. The argument is based on the belief that courts should not substitute their own points of view for the policy judgments of the "democratic" branches of government—legislative and executive. If this meant nothing more than that judges should be careful, few would quarrel with it; the worst blows to the Court, historically, have been in instances in which it has forgotten the strict limitations on its power: cases such as the *Dred Scott Case* or the New Deal series. But as we have already seen, there is no possible way, given the ambiguity of the constitutional text and the grave policy implications of constitutional cases, by which judges can decide such cases without deciding at the same time—at least implicitly—the policy questions involved. Even self-restraint ends up as an implicit approval of a policy. (It should be noted that the general public is very likely to misunderstand what policy has been approved. When Justice Frankfurter votes to uphold the flag-salute requirement, the public draws the conclusion that he approves of the flag salute, because this is the policy that results from the decision. The fact is, however, that he does not approve of the flag salute; what he does approve is the theory that the state should have the right to decide whether or not to require a flag salute. And this approval is grounded on a theory of democracy, of federalism, and of judicial power. In this sense Frankfurter's opinions are just as much an expression of his own philosophy and preferences as those of any activist. In other words, one of the crosses an apostle of self-restraint must bear is the public's misunderstanding of what policy he is upholding.)

Any decision is inevitably political; even the refusal to make a decision is political. The point may be illustrated, if it is not already

---

[1] *West Virginia State Board of Education v. Barnette*, 319 U.S. 624 (1943).
[2] *Times Film Corp v. Chicago*, 365 U.S. 43 (1961).
[3] *Reynolds v. United States*, 98 U.S. 145 (1879).

clear, by reference to the 1961 case involving the Vermont practice of paying tuition of students to parochial high schools in areas where there were no public schools. The practice had been found unconstitutional by the Vermont Supreme Court. The United States Supreme Court refused to review the case.[4] Legally, such refusal implies nothing except that the Court felt it had better ways to spend its time. But politically it meant at least two very important things, and the justices were fully aware of both of them. First, it meant that the decision of the Vermont court stands as the law, at least in Vermont; it will probably be influential in other states as well. Second, it meant, in the context of the political argument over federal aid to parochial schools which was raging at the time, that the general public, even including lawyers, would regard the Court's inaction as a sign that a majority of the judges would regard federal aid as unconstitutional. The judges' silence spoke almost as loud as a decision would have, although not as clearly. And tactically, the Supreme Court left itself free to make any decision it might wish in case a similar case is accepted in the future. These "political" considerations, possibly unspoken in judicial conference, were nevertheless very present in the minds of the justices, and perhaps had much to do with the decision *not* to decide. And who can say which man is the more political: the judge who wanted to take the case and decide it (either way), or the judge who wanted to avoid the issue?

The difference between the "self-restraintist" and the "activist" is thus something short of fundamental. The really fundamental cleavage is, as it has always been, between those who favor judicial review as an institution and those who wish to be without it. For any court with the power of judicial review is inevitably political; the only way to "get the Supreme Court out of politics" is to abolish its power to declare acts of government unconstitutional. Objectivity or neutrality in constitutional issues is a chimera; the search for it, however necessary, is fruitless.

If the basic question is judicial review itself, what may we conclude as to its desirability in the American scheme of government? Many of the arguments in its favor (and against it) have been canvassed in the first two chapters. The viewpoint of this text may be briefly summarized by repeating that the American concept of government has always been one of *limited* government; the rise of democracy in the mid-nineteenth century did not signify a revulsion against these limits. Indeed, part of the motivation for democracy in the English-speaking world has been the feeling that governmental limitations are safer in the hands of the people than in those of an elite or an absolute monarch. It is almost axiomatic that the Bill of Rights contains a statement of the major limitations in which we have believed. It does

---

[4] *Anderson* v. *Swart*, 81 S.Ct. 1349 (1961); certiorari denied.

not seem unreasonable for a court to require the government to observe these limitations so long as they remain in the Constitution. One may agree that public opinion rules in the long run, without asking the Supreme Court to abdicate in the short run.

In sum, those liberals who in the 1930's and earlier attacked the whole institution of judicial review were mistaking the forest for the trees; in their disagreement with a particular line of decisions they made the mistake of wishing to abandon an accepted, useful, and on the whole desirable part of our political system.

Politics and the Selection of Judges

In the above context, it may be useful to return to the subject of the selection of judges, which we have already discussed in Chapter V. This is always a subject of some controversy. For many years the various bar associations have been claiming a right to influence appointments, and there have been many criticisms of the excessively "political" appointments made by presidents as far separated in time as Jefferson and Truman. Presidents are often exhorted to appoint to the highest court only judges with substantial experience on lower courts, and President Eisenhower followed this practice in his last four appointments. And even more recently, in 1961, President Kennedy pledged himself to look for appointees "with respected professional skill, incorruptible character, firm judicial temperament, the rare inner quality to know when to temper justice with mercy and the intellectual capacity to protect and illuminate the Constitution and our historic values in the context of a society experiencing profound and rapid change." [5]

There is nothing specifically wrong with such criteria: a man on the bench with all of the qualities called for by Kennedy would be a paragon of virtue. However, he would not necessarily be a great Supreme Court justice, although Kennedy has probably come closer than most political leaders to identifying the qualities that make for greatness in such a position. The point is, or should be, obvious: the Supreme Court is not only, or even primarily, a court of law; it is, on the contrary, an extremely significant working part of our political system. The great judge, therefore, requires some of the qualities of a statesman in addition to those of a lawyer. Judicial statesmanship is not the same thing as legal craftsmanship.

It is for this reason that judges from lower courts, even good judges, are no more likely to be good Supreme Court justices than politicians with no previous judicial experience. In fact the work of all lower courts is different not only in degree but even in kind from

---

[5] As quoted in *New York Times*, May 20, 1961, p. 8.

the work of the Supreme Court. Such a perceptive judge as Benjamin Cardozo, who served both on the highest court of New York and on the United States Supreme Court, has testified that his twenty years as a judge proved almost totally irrelevant to the problems that he faced on the Supreme Court. Any list of the twelve or fifteen men who have been the "best" to serve on the Supreme Court would illustrate the lack of correspondence between success on the Court and previous success either on lower courts or as a practicing lawyer. Non-lawyers are sometimes even tempted to the heretical (and probably false) belief that legal training has little or nothing to do with the kind of justices we obtain. (Since all Supreme Court justices have been trained in the law, there is no way to test this belief empirically; but lawyers make a strong case that the habits of discipline, the train-ing in research and in logical thinking which are part of legal educa-tion are indispensable to a judge at any level.) A President in making his appointments requires more in the way of prescience than is com-mon among men, if he is to pick successfully those candidates who have "the rare inner quality to know when to temper justice with mercy and the intellectual capacity to protect and illuminate the Constitution and our historic values in the context of a society ex-periencing profound and rapid change." There is precious little that we can be sure of in a man's career that will provide a reliable guide as to his possession of these desirable commodities, or (more to the point) his ability to use them on the Supreme Court bench. The great judges of the period 1900 to 1937, for instance, were Holmes, Brandeis, Hughes, Cardozo, and perhaps Sutherland, Taft, and Stone. Of these, three had long judicial careers before reaching the Court (Holmes, Cardozo, and Taft); the others were lawyer-politicians, or, in the case of Brandeis, simply a lawyer. It may parenthetically be said that few observers in 1915 would have thought that Brandeis possessed that elusive thing called "a judicial temperament"; and the same was true of Stone. The dominant figures on the Court since 1937 have undoubtedly been Frankfurter, Black, and Douglas, none of whom ever sat as a judge before his swearing in as a Supreme Court justice.

It is likely that the decision whether a particular judge is "great" rests with the judgment of history: it is an ex post facto judgment which seemingly is based to a great extent on the individual's ability to ride the wave of the future in his decisions. The reason Holmes is considered great while Sutherland is largely ignored lies at least partly in Holmes's accord with the future and Sutherland's contrasting effort to stay the hand of time.

One may be pardoned, then, for wondering whether a President is well advised to pay too much attention to the mere fact that a man has been a judge. In fact, it seems likely that Southern leaders who make this argument (and perhaps also the American Bar Association) are attempting through the use of such specific qualifications to influence not the quality of judges but rather the kind of decisions. Southerners are somewhat in the habit of following this thought pattern: the school segregation decision is contrary to the real meaning of the Constitution; thus it must be that the judges who made it are either (1) poor judges and/or (2) politicians on the bench. The decision thus becomes that horror of horrors, "a political decision"; the moral then drawn is that the way to prevent such decisions is to make sure that "politicians" do not get to the bench, but only trained judges, who presumably would not make such mistakes. The fact that the trained judges on the Court went along with the segregation decision is conveniently ignored. But the significant thing is that, even if the critics had their way, it would probably make little or no difference in the course of decisions; it might improve to some extent the quality of opinion-writing, though even this is doubtful.

If one wished to try to predict what kind of decisions a man would make, he would have to know at least three things. First, one would need to know what kind of cases would be most likely to be important during the candidate's tenure. This can be guessed at but not predicted with any certainty. Second, one would wish to know as much as possible about the candidate's judicial philosophy, that is, his ideas of the proper role of the Supreme Court in our polity. This would be possible in some cases but probably not in most, for many appointees do not articulate their philosophies until there is a need to do so; and some justices never do so. It would thus have been possible to predict Felix Frankfurter's ideal of judgeship, for he had written of it extensively long before his appointment. But very few people read it closely and consequently many were surprised at the kind of judge he became. On the other hand, Black had never articulated a judicial philosophy, and his only became apparent as he was faced with day-to-day cases. Perhaps most run-of-the-mill justices (say, Roberts or Van Devanter) have played it by ear, usually with the result that their economic philosophies governed rather than any clearly thought-out theory of the judicial function. And finally, one would need to know a good deal about the candidate's strength of will, for many judges turn out to be "followers" who take their cues from one or another of the men who are dominant on the bench during their tenures. A Court consisting entirely of great judges might turn out to be pretty hard to live with; as readers will already know, the amount of independent thinking on the post-1937 Supreme Court has resulted in a level of internal disagreement which has deeply concerned many observers. But one would hesitate to conclude from this that a President should deliberately look for a certain number of "followers" on the bench. In any event, how would one know whom they would follow?

Conclusion

This excursion into the politics of appointment has been made with the aim of emphasizing the central point of this book: that the Supreme Court is both more and less than a court of law, and that its methods and functions cannot be judged solely from the standpoint of the law. This is why constitutional law is a course in the political science curriculum.

Some commentators, conceding this point, nevertheless view with some reservations the idea that the ordinary layman should be taught that the Court is in and of politics. They are fearful that a public so enlightened would see no use for the Court in its traditional role. The argument seems to be that the Court can act effectively in its political role as constitutional watchdog only when the general public thinks of that role as being legal, not political. For if the Court is "political," in what way is it attending to any task that cannot be performed more democratically by the representative branches of the government? There is much force to the question, particularly if the public has only a little knowledge: a little knowledge is as dangerous in this field as in any other. The function of a constitutional law course is to help students to attain a deeper knowledge which will carry them beyond the superficial cynicism about the Court which might otherwise result.

We have argued, then, that the Court is political. But we have also argued that its role in politics is necessary and desirable; that it performs its functions in a way that could not be equalled by any *merely* political agency; and that, on the whole, American history tends to validate this role of the Court in a democracy. It cannot, indeed, save us from ourselves if we are determined on national democratic suicide; but it can perhaps provide the still, small voice of conscience and the second-thought consideration which may dissuade us from such a reckless course. If this is a far cry from judicial supremacy, it is important enough to induce a sobering sense of responsibility on most judges. If, on the other hand, it is far from direct democracy, it occurs within a total framework of democracy which validates it as a part of a working, pragmatic, rather than ideal, institution.

Suggestions for Further Reading

It should be apparent to the reader of this book that many of the citations contained in previous chapters traverse the general questions that we have tried to summarize in this concluding chapter. The reader is therefore referred back to the earlier citations for much of the comment on this subject. There are, nevertheless, a good many publications which are not specialized enough to have been mentioned earlier, or which concentrate on contemporary areas of controversy concerning the Court and its role. These are listed here.

Books

Commager, Henry Steele. *Majority Rule and Minority Rights* (Gloucester, Mass.: Peter Smith, 1950); a defense of majority rule unchecked by judicial review.

Frank, Jerome. *Law and the Modern Mind* (New York: Coward-McCann, 1949); a psychological approach to the problem of judging.

Frankfurter, Felix. *Of Law and Men* (New York: Harcourt, Brace & Co., 1956); a collection of occasional essays.

Jackson, Robert H. *The Supreme Court in the American System of Government* (Cambridge: Harvard University Press, 1955); lectures by a distinguished Supreme Court justice.

McWhinney, Edward. *Judicial Review in the English-Speaking World* (Toronto: University of Toronto Press, 1956); a comparative study.

Mendelson, Wallace. *Justices Black and Frankfurter: Conflict on the Court* (Chicago: University of Chicago Press, 1961); a defense of Frankfurter's doctrine of judicial self-restraint.

Powell, Thomas Reed. *Vagaries and Varieties in Constitutional Interpretation* (New York: Columbia University Press, 1956); occasional essays by a great teacher.

Pritchett, C. Herman. *Civil Liberties and the Vinson Court* (Chicago: University of Chicago Press, 1954); an analysis of the divisions on the Court during Vinson's tenure.

―――. *The Political Offender and the Warren Court* (Boston: Boston University Press, 1958); an analysis of the Warren Court's record to 1957.

Roberts, Owen J. *The Court and the Constitution* (Cambridge: Harvard University Press, 1951); post-retirement reflections by the pivotal justice in the 1937 "switch in time that saved nine."

Warren, Charles. *Congress, the Constitution and the Supreme Court* (Boston: Little, Brown & Co., 1935); a conservative defense of the Supreme Court.

Articles

Beth, Loren P. "The Supreme Court and the Future of Judicial Review," 76 *Pol. Sci. Qtrly.* 11 (1961).

Braden, George D. "The Search for Objectivity in Constitutional Law," 57 *Yale Law Jnl.* 571 (1948).

Irish, Marian. "Mr. Justice Douglas and Judicial Restraint," 6 *Univ. of Florida Law Rev.* 537 (1953).

Lancaster, Robert S. "Judge Learned Hand and the Limits of Judicial Discretion," 9 *Vanderbilt Law Rev.* 427 (1956).

McKay, Robert B. "The Supreme Court and Its Lawyer Critics," 28 *Fordham Law Rev.* 615 (1959–60).

McWhinney, Edward. "The Supreme Court and the Dilemma of Judicial Policy-Making," 39 *Minnesota Law Rev.* 837 (1955).
———. "The Great Debate: Activism and Self-Restraint and Current Dilemmas in Judicial Policy-Making," 33 *New York Univ. Law Qtrly.* 775 (1958).
Mendelson, Wallace. "Mr. Justice Frankfurter and the Process of Judicial Review," 103 *Univ. of Pennsylvania Law Rev.* 295 (1954).
Menez, Joseph F. "A Brief in Support of the Supreme Court," 54 *Northwestern Univ. Law Rev.* 30 (1959).
Miller, Arthur S., and Howell, Ronald F. "The Myth of Neutrality in Constitutional Adjudication," 27 *Univ. of Chicago Law Rev.* 661 (1960).
Murphy, Walter F. "Mr. Justice Jackson, Free Speech, and the Judicial Function," 12 *Vanderbilt Law Rev.* 1019 (1959).
Steamer, Robert J. "Statesmanship or Craftsmanship: Current Conflict over the Supreme Court," 11 *Western Pol. Qtrly.* 265 (1958).
Wechsler, Herbert. "Toward Neutral Principles of Constitutional Law," 73 *Harvard Law Rev.* 1 (1959).
Symposium: "Mr. Justice Black," 65 *Yale Law Jnl.* 449 (1956).
Symposium: "Policy-Making in a Democracy: The Role of the United States Supreme Court," 6 *Jnl. of Public Law* 275 (1957).
Symposium: "The Role of the Supreme Court in the American Constitutional System," 33 *Notre Dame Lawyer* 521 (1958).

Notes on the
Study of
Constitutional Law

A profitable study of constitutional law will include a good deal of attention to legal philosophy and a knowledge of the American political system—two subjects which have been surveyed but briefly in this book. But it is also important to study cases and to familiarize oneself with at least some of the current comment about them. The present section aims to give some of the rudiments which may help in the use of the "tools" of study.

Case Reports

All federal appellate and many district court decisions and opinions are formally reported in volumes available in any law school and some university libraries. Supreme Court decisions may be found in the *United States Reports* (or, before the year 1874, the reports issued under the names of the various court reporters). Somewhat more useful at times are the two privately published sets of Supreme Court reports, *The Supreme Court Reporter* and the *Lawyers' Edition*. A privately published set of reports for the lower federal courts is also available; it has gone under various titles but at present is published as two sets, *Federal Reporter* (2d series) for circuit court decisions, and the *Federal Supplement* for the district courts. There are reports for the appellate decisions of the state courts, published separately for each state; in addition a private publisher puts out regional volumes which comprise the appellate decisions of the state courts in the various regions of the country.

There is a uniform system of citing cases so that any reader may find them easily. It consists of the volume, name, page, and date—in that order. Consequently, the *Dred Scott Case* is cited: *Scott* v. *Sandford*, 19 How.[for Howard] 393 (1857). "U.S." means United States Reports; "S.Ct.," Supreme Court Reporter; "L. Ed.," Lawyers' Edition. "F (2d)" stands for Federal Reporter (2d series), while "F. Supp." means Federal Supplement.

It should be noted that in a case system of law the case reports are the basic materials of study. No study of constitutional law is complete if the student has not acquainted himself with case materials and how to use them. Students in colleges that do not have the reports described above will probably find a casebook of value. There are over a dozen casebooks now in publication for both law school and political science courses. Most of them are adequate in the provision of the opinions from the most important constitutional law decisions, but they vary widely in their editing and completeness. The student is cautioned to use the original reports if possible, because they are not cut or edited, and they include all the concurring and dissenting opinions, which the casebooks often leave out.

Other Study Materials

Case studies give the raw material. Perspective, however, can only be acquired either through more case study than the student can perform, or by the reading of other materials. This text is such a broadening device. In addition, there are hundreds of books published on various phases of constitutional law, some of which are doubtless on every instructor's reading list for his course. Current materials may be found in the various law reviews, political science journals, and in some more popular publications. In order to use these, however, one must be familiar with the indexes. The political science journals are indexed primarily in the *Public Affairs Information Service* index; popular publications are indexed in *Readers' Guide* (also, the *New York Times* and its *Index* are invaluable for current reports). Law reviews are separately indexed in the *Index to Legal Periodicals* and the *Law Review Digest*.

Analyzing a Case

Despite what has just been said, the mere reading of a case is not very enlightening. It is important to have some idea of what to look for in the case, and to acquire the knack of reading between the lines of the opinions. In addition, to a political scientist a case is meaningless out of its political context: the student should know why the case is important, its political, social, and economic background, the implications of its disposition, and the probable reactions of various groups to the decision. Such knowledge can only be obtained by a great deal of reading or a thorough training in political science and American history. Since this course cannot give all such background, obviously much depends on the initiative of the student if he is to receive maximum benefit from his study. All that can be done here is to provide a few pointers in how to get the most out of case reading.

For purposes of nonlegal study, case analysis should properly concentrate on what the issue of public concern is, how it is settled in the court action, and why the settlement was made the way it was. The technicalities are often valuable and important but for our purposes not as basic. In making a written case analysis, then, make sure that the analysis answers the three basic questions mentioned. Finally, some personal evaluation of the import of the case should be added to the analysis, as well as your own criticism or praise of the opinions, and any other comment on the case that seems significant. Most of the space in a case analysis is taken up by the summary of reasoning contained in the opinions. Be sure to include *all* the opinions, and in your personal comments it is valuable to include a statement of which of the opinions you think is most valid.

As may be gathered, the supposition here is that each student will actually write out a full case analysis for each case that is assigned for reading by the instructor. While your instructor may not ask you to hand such analyses in, yet they will be valuable in forcing you to pin down your thoughts on a case and make sure you really understand it, and they will be very useful in review studies for exams or for use in exams if your instructor allows their use. Obviously, no one else's case analysis will be as valuable to you as your own.

A Sample Case Analysis

Below is presented a sample analysis of a case which may serve as a model. It is a relatively simple case chosen more or less at random.

TOOLSON *v.* NEW YORK YANKEES
346 U.S. 356, 74 S.Ct. 78 (1953)

Three cases from two different district courts, in which baseball players sued under the federal antitrust laws; players were refused relief in all cases, and appealed to circuit courts, which also denied relief. Supreme Court granted certiorari.

The Issue: Is professional baseball included in the scope of the federal antitrust laws?

THE ANSWER: No.

THE OPINION: *Per curiam*. A previous case (1922) held baseball not subject to antitrust regulation. Congress after that decision did not legislate to bring it under the laws. The precedent case is followed. "If there are evils in this field which now warrant application to it of the antitrust laws it should be by legislation."

DISSENTING OPINION: Justice Burton (with Clark). The Court is wrong in holding that baseball is not interstate commerce. Data given to prove that it is. The Court has misread the precedent case, for it did not say Congress had excluded baseball from regulation; it said baseball was not interstate commerce and thus could not be regulated by Congress. Congress has enacted no exemption of baseball, and no implied exemption has been shown.

COMMENT: The dissent seems closer to reality than the majority opinion, both in its reading of the precedent and in its reading of the meaning of Congressional silence. Also note that the Court has later in three cases held other entertainment businesses subject to antitrust regulation: the legitimate theater, boxing and professional football, distinguishing them rather unconvincingly from this case.

QUERY: Since the recent transcontinental moves and expansions of the major leagues, would the justices be able today to regard baseball as entertainment rather than commerce?

Limitations of Case Analysis

In analyzing cases, it should be borne in mind that the case, read by itself and in isolation, seems more purely legal than it usually is in reality. The regulation of baseball, for instance, has been debated in Congress several times, and has been a bone of contention between the players and the owners. It is a political and economic question of some importance. But none of this appears in the opinion of the Court, and only by indirection in the dissenting opinion. As noted earlier, court opinions are often as significant for what they do not say as they are for what they do say. The motivations of judges do not usually appear explicitly; policy considerations are often unmentioned. The dissent in the *Toolson Case* accuses the majority of showing a sentimental partiality for baseball—but from mere reading one can get no such impression from the majority opinion. A case, to be intelligently handled, must be viewed in the light of such intangible elements. That this involves guesswork with the consequent risk of error does not absolve the student from the responsibility of trying to make intelligent guesses.

Index

78–79; plain meaning of, 88–89; intentions of framers, 89–90; and common law, 93; endangered by Depression, 111–12; interpretation during New Deal, 117; broadened interpretation of, 126–27; and economic theory, 142; restrictive and expansive possibilities of, 142; on civil liberties, 143, 152–53; nature of interpretation of, 150–51

Constitutionalism, 2–25, 44, 127
Constitutionality, 83–84, 95–96
Constitutions, written, 8, 10–12, 138
Contract clause, 140
Convention, constitutional, 132, 134
Conventions, state ratifying, 134
Cooley, Thomas M., 72
Coolidge, Calvin, 115
Corwin, Edward S., 138
Court-packing, 86–87, 121–27
Courts of Appeals, U.S.: See **Appeals**, U.S. Circuit Courts of
Courts, legislative, 29
Courts, state, 29, 31–33
Courts, territorial, 29
Courts, U.S. District, 29, 101
Crosskey, W. W., 89
Cummings, Homer S., 121
Curtis, Charles P., 149

Davis, David, 100
Decision, court, 42–43, 87–96
Declaratory Judgment Act, federal, 36
Delegation of legislative power, 117–20, 126
Democracy, 17–19, 22–25
Democratic party, 19, 97–100, 113, 129
Despotism, 4
De Tocqueville, Alexis, 17–18, 84–85; quoted, 5, 57
Dickinson, John, 134
Discretion of courts, 33, 35–39, 52–53, 68–71, 79, 92, 96, 148–55
District courts, U.S. See Courts, U.S. District
Dollar devaluation, 118–19
Dooley, Mr., 85
Dorr's Rebellion, 38
Douglas, William O., 36, 48, 81, 128–29, 143
Due process of law, 33, 62–64, 78, 143, 145
Due process of law, substantive. See Substantive due process of law

Eastland, James O., 100
Edgerton, Henry, 48
Eisenhower, Dwight D., 99, 153
Eleventh Amendment, 78
Elizabeth I, Queen of England, 6
Ellsworth, Oliver, 134, 136
Enforcement powers, lack of, 81–82
England: 132–33; constitutionalism in, 4–8, 12, 18–21; courts in, 64, 149
Enumerated powers, 13
Ethics, judicial, 64–65, 81, 83, 137
Evidence, rules of, 64
Exhaustion of remedy doctrine, 37
Ex post facto laws, 21

Fair Labor Standards Act, 60–61, 126–27
Fair trial, 12, 33, 64, 94
Federal Power Commission, 92–93
Federal system, 11, 13, 16–17
Federal Trade Commission, 119
Federalist party, 66, 135–38
Federalist, The, 1, 16, 134, 138
Field, Stephen J., 40, 86, 94, 105–7
Fifteenth Amendment, 20
First Amendment, 96
Flag salute, 92, 151
Florida Supreme Court, 43
Football, professional, 162
Fourteenth Amendment, 33, 66, 78, 95
Framers' intentions, 89–90
France, 4
Frankfurter, Felix, 32, 37, 47, 72, 92, 99, 102, 104, 107, 128–29, 143, 150–52, 155; quoted, 27, 51
Franklin, Benjamin, 134
Frazier-Lemke Act, 119
Freedom: of religion; of speech, 12. See *also* Bill of Rights; Civil liberties
French Revolution, 64
Frontier, influence of on judges, 114
Fuller, Melville, 105

Georgia, 139–40
Germanic law, 4
Gerry, Elbridge, 134
"GI" Bill, 61
Gladstone, William E., 9
Glass, Carter, 101
Grant, Ulysses S., 87, 99
Gray, Horace, 107
Great Britain. See England
Greece, 2–3, 5
Guffey Coal Act, 65–66, 121

Habeas Corpus Act of 1867, 87
Habeas corpus, writ of, 32–33, 64, 82
Haines, Charles Grove, 134, 136
Hamilton, Alexander, 1, 10, 16, 69, 117, 134–35, 138
Hamilton, Walton H., 44, 107–8
Hand, Augustus N., 51
Hand, Learned, 51–52; quoted 13
Harding, Warren G., 113
Harlan, John Marshall, 40, 48, 100–101, 104, 106–7, 112
Hatch Act, 36
Hayes, Rutherford B., 100–101
Hitler, Adolf, 64
Holmes, Oliver Wendell, 46, 48, 62–63, 81, 91, 96–98, 102, 104, 107, 112–14, 128, 150, 154
Hoover, Herbert C., 98, 115–16
Hot Oil Case, 117–18
House of Representatives, U.S., 11
Hughes, Charles Evans, 45–47, 61, 104–7, 113, 115–19, 121–25, 129, 154

Immigration officials, 61
Implied meaning, 88–89
Implied powers, 13, 117
Income tax amendment, 78
Income Tax Case, 40, 66–67
Incompetence, judicial, 92–93